TOUCHED BY FIRE

TOUCHED BY FIRE

A Photographic Portrait of the Civil War

VOLUME TWO

★ ★

William C. Davis   EDITOR

William A. Frassanito   PHOTOGRAPHIC CONSULTANT

A Project of The National Historical Society

LITTLE, BROWN AND COMPANY   Boston   Toronto

FIRST EDITION

Library of Congress Cataloging-in-Publication Data
(Revised for volume 2)

Touched by fire.

   "A project of the National Historical Society."
   Includes indexes.
   1. United States — History — Civil War, 1861–1865 —
Pictorial works.   I. Davis, William C., 1946-
II. Frassanito, William A.   III. National Historical
Society.
E468.7.T68   1985   973.7′022′2   85-12967
ISBN 0-316-17661-3 (v. 1)
ISBN 0-316-17664-8 (v. 2)

HAL

Designed by Patricia Girvin Dunbar

Published simultaneously in Canada
by Little, Brown & Company (Canada) Limited

PRINTED IN THE UNITED STATES OF AMERICA

Contents

Introduction   *William C. Davis*   3

E Pluribus Duo   Harold M. Hyman   5

Feeding the Machine   *Maury Klein*   37

Camp Nelson: Mr. Lincoln's Microcosm   *A Portfolio*   87

Fire and Stone   *Robert K. Krick*   111

Billy Yank   *A Portfolio*   159

Everyone's War   *Emory M. Thomas*   199

The Ravages of War   *Stephen B. Oates*   237

The War to Posterity   *A Portfolio*   295

Contributors   327

Photograph Credits   328

Index   329

TOUCHED BY FIRE

Introduction
William C. Davis

OF ALL THE HUMAN SENSES, none opens to us so much of wonder and fascination as sight; none can so move our feelings and emotions for good or ill. It could hardly be a surprise, then, that the world went a bit camera-happy when the discovery of photographic processes in the last century opened, to millions around the globe, vistas of scenes unseen, places unvisited, and experiences undreamed. Hardly surprising is it, either, that the first epic human endeavor to occur after the camera's development should become one of the most photographed events in modern times. The camera and the American Civil War were like children of the same generation, linked in a sibling relationship that produced not rivalry but a profound partnership and a moving documentary record of a people who were literally "touched by fire."

The first volume of this work addressed much of that human experience — its impact upon the continent, upon the leaders and the led, the story of the lasting compact of comradeship that the war experience produced, the face of the Confederate soldier, and more. This second volume of *Touched by Fire* continues the story, its purpose the same. This is no definitive history. For the scholars and serious armchair historians, there will perhaps be little that is truly new in the text on the pages that follow. But this is not intended to be a new history of the war.

Rather, *Touched by Fire* attempts in this volume, as in its predecessor, to present some specific themes that run through Civil War history, in ways that most of the public — and not a few historians — will not have considered before. Just what was the nature of the two governments that waged war upon one another? Where were their ideologies divergent, and how did they reflect the aspirations of the peoples who supported them? Some penetrating thoughts in response to those questions appear herein. So many books have been written about the armies and what they did. But how much does the public know of the virtual armies of the unseen and unheralded, those behind-the-lines support services without which no army in any age could move? And what of the role of minorities in this war? After all, the chief catalyst for the conflict was America's most visible minority, the slaves. Yet they were only one of many ethnic and racial groups who made this terrible experience their war too.

There is much more. The Civil War revolutionized infantry weapons and tactics. Less recognized is what it did to the sciences of defensive fortifications and artillery, two features of conflict most readily identified with warfare. This volume offers some insights into the revolution that occurred in these areas, too, and why. We look at the face of Billy Yank, that indomitable soldier whose resolve lasted through years of defeat and setback before he marched onward to final victory. And we see the terrible cost of the war in the waste it laid on the people and their landscape.

While the text tells much, the photographs, which attract and capture the eye, are what really illuminate this vision. Of the 542 images in this volume, more than half have not been published previously. At that, they represent only the tiniest, almost incalculable, fraction of the total photographic legacy of the war. Alas, the cameras could not be everywhere, and there were many scenes, many experiences of the war, that were simply never captured on negatives. In many cases, so few images survive — sometimes only a single one — that in order to provide any coverage at all, we must rely upon views already published many times over. We are fortunate to have them, though, for like a fine piece of music, they get better with every new "performance."

That we have images like these to present is due to many individuals and institutions. Fortunately, those who came before us, now long dead, had a sense of history. They knew that these fading views carried a memory of a generation and a time that would be everlasting in the consciousness of the American people. These were shadows of the past worth saving, and tens of thousands of them have been saved. It took a few years after the war for government to appreciate their worth, but in time it did. Meanwhile, collectors and antiquarians had already begun the work of preservation, as they continue it today. Would all these images have survived had they not related to a subject that itself remains the most written about and talked about event in our history? Probably, for the vision of the Civil War is often more persuasive than the narratives. Indeed, it is the photographs themselves that have led many of the uninitiated to their first exploration of a topic that has captured them for life.

Without those institutions and collectors, we could not present this or any other volume. They deserve recognition for what they are doing to help people remember — but lists of names in book introductions are little read, and less recollected. That is human nature, so anxious are we to *see* what there is to follow. (Indeed, introductions themselves are little read, and that is all right.) Few collectors maintain these priceless old images in order to achieve recognition. They acquire and save them because they must. It is a calling — a compulsion to see as much as possible for themselves, and to preserve for the rest of us. The surety that they have done this is often thanks enough.

In looking at these remarkable views, in learning the lessons they impart, in remembering what they represent, we thank also those who made them — and those who suffered and sacrificed and triumphed and failed while the images were being made. Seeing these scenes now, as they may only be seen in these pages, we can still feel the flames that touched their lives.

E Pluribus Duo

★ ★

Harold M. Hyman

O̲ur Civil War was many wars. Above all else, it was a civil war. History's verdict is that civil wars unleash the worst behavior of individuals and governments and profoundly deteriorate the standards of the warring societies, especially if a conflict continues for a long time, and most especially when racial or religious factors are involved. In the 1850s, during the Taiping Rebellion, Chinese killed probably 20 million other Chinese. Ten years later, Frenchmen so savagely suppressed the Paris Commune uprising as to inspire Georges Clemenceau (who as a journalist had reported from Washington on our Civil War and Reconstruction) to note sadly that in France half the nation was a firing squad for the losing half. From 1917 to 1920, the Russian Revolution created perhaps 10 million civilian casualties. And no reliable casualty estimates exist for the post–World War II civil wars in China, Vietnam, India — the list is long.

America's Civil War became the longest one fought anywhere in the Western world during the period between Napoleon's surrender in 1815 and World War I. It involved the intertwined destinies of whole races. Yet with rare exceptions Union and Confederate armies obeyed "laws" of war that, elsewhere, did not apply in civil wars. Despite the fact that the nineteenth century was the classic time of "men-on-horseback" military dictators seizing power out of civil wars, in our Civil War civilians retained tight control over the bestarred galaxy. When the Civil War ended, the victor did not impose mass executions, exilings, jailings, or property confiscations. Disfranchisements were few and brief. Indeed, our Reconstruction, both before and after Appomattox, was a sustained attempt to increase, not decrease, the electorates of the would-be Confederate states. The major characteristics of the restored Union of states — constitutionalism, federalism, and biracial democracy — were far better based than when the war began.

Our Civil War was surprising in that it occurred at all. In the winter of 1860/61, odds were very heavy against the United States fighting to save itself. Northern timidity in the face of rising demands by Southern whites for favored treatment had begun in 1787. Responsively, the Constitution's framers had substantially overrepresented the Southern states in the House of Representatives and the electoral college by counting each slave as three-fifths of a person, and had also yielded by specifying as a federal duty the return of fugitive slaves even from nonslave states. Then, in historic "compromises" of 1820, 1850, and 1854, concerning slavery in the national territories (future states), this tradition of giving in to the South received spectacular reemphases.

Despite these political successes, Southerners grew ever-more fearful for their special property rights in humans. After the November 1860 election of Republican candidate Abraham Lincoln to be president, the Deep South's leaders organized their states' secessions from the Union. Lame-duck president James Buchanan could find no relevant constitutional grounds or military resources for halting the outgoing tide. Unopposed state secessions further convinced Southerners that urban and commercial corruptions, non-English (that is, Irish, German, and free Negro) immigrants, and excessively open political democracy had made the nonslave North impotent. Only weeks after Lincoln's inauguration, in April 1861, Confederate president Jefferson Davis ordered the artillery attack that quickly forced the surrender of the tiny garrison on one of the nation's last Atlantic strongholds in the South, Fort Sumter in Charleston.

Was Sumter's surrender the Union's last leaf? Many commentators here and abroad thought that obituaries were in order. No nation that fails to protect its military property in one of its own harbors was likely to outlast even the strains of peace, much less fight a war. Should a war come, however, the Confederacy, it appeared obvious even to amateur strategists, enjoyed large advantages. The East Coast's complex mountain-to-Atlantic rivers were ideal for defense, especially with hordes of docile slave-laborers to dig trenches and erect fortifications. Southerners also saw correctly that the Confederacy needed to win no battles — although it would. Instead, the Confederates, like their Revolutionary fathers before them, had to hold out against a superior foe until they won by default.

Soon after Appomattox yearners after the Lost Cause created a tradition that the Confederacy could never have won, that the Union's industrial, communications, and population advantages foredoomed the South to defeat. The tradition is still impressive, especially if statistics are seen as a primary measure of history. Union states numbered twenty-two or twenty-three, depending on whether West Virginia is counted. Throughout the war years, European immigrants reinforced the Union's 22 million residents. Telegraph, factory, and farm figures were all six to seven times greater in the North than in Secessia, and except along the Maryland-through-Missouri border, the unseceded states were little disturbed by actual combat. Washington possessed foreign recognition, functioning credit and fiscal structures, and existing government institutions.

By contrast, at peak the Confederate states numbered only eleven (plus two "rump" states), had but 9 million residents (of whom more than one-third were black), and saw virtually no immigration. The South had to create its national government institutions since it abandoned those the Union provided. And foreign recognition never came. But, to balance, the South had significant natural resources and industrial-communications facilities. Its agricultural output was magnificent. Slave labor served farms, factories, mines, and, as laborers, the Confederate armies. Because the endless, twisted Atlantic and Gulf coasts and the Mexican border were unblockadable, waves of goods flowed into the South.

Less precise data may be ultimately more significant in assessing civil wars, as the poet W. H. Auden advised when he warned: "Never sit with statisticians nor commit a social science." Agricultural societies lacking great cities are like sponge rubber to invading armies, whose battlefield successes can seem to be meaningless while the defenders' armies remain alive. The Union, not the Confederacy, had to invade and to garrison a region larger than all Europe west of the Rhine; had to win gory campaigns, not single battles; had to recreate the governments of thirteen states and of a multitude of localities — all in the face of overwhelmingly hostile white residents — before it could even approach the war aim of 1861, national reunion.

Adding to the South's advantages was the fact that Southern white society did not suffer the "excesses of democracy" of two-party politics in Union states. Thinking in these terms, Lincoln used rural imagery. He pictured himself as a (not *the*) driver of a frail wagon — the Union. Ahead, pulling the cart, were three powerful horses in tandem. All moved toward one common goal, reunion, but not at the same speed. In the lead, trying to gallop, was the so-called radical Republican, who wanted reunion plus abolition of slavery. The second horse, the "regular" Republican, was content only to canter, and was less sure about emancipation. Last of the three, the "war" Democrat, wanted reunion only, but might be convinced that emancipation was essential, and yet would only trot ahead. But tied behind the wagon was the antiwar, pro-Southern, Negrophobe Democrat, heels dug in to retard any forward motion. Could the weary, creaking Union-wagon long endure such torsions?

By contrast, the Confederate condition was one of overwhelming white unity favoring a war to retain existing race relationships. The South was composed, politically, of single-party or no-party states. Only prowar Democratic organizations existed, except for a few antique, irrelevant Whig remnants. No Republican organizations polluted any seceded state. To be sure, in scattered border localities in western Virginia, Missouri, Tennessee, and Texas, some antisecession and anti-slavery sentiment coexisted with white-superiority convictions. But until secession and war created the opportunities in the form of "invading" Bluecoats, such sentiment rarely generated politically meaningful organization or strength. In slave states law and custom had combined, long before the Civil War, to locate and stifle dissent, whether through legal procedures or the "hanging tree." Consider that United States senator Andrew Johnson of Tennessee had to flee his state in 1861 in order to escape being assaulted or even lynched, returning to it a year later in the wake of Union troopers as Lincoln's military governor. In short, the South gave off an illusion of massive white unity.

It was no illusion that most Southerners, even including many antisecessionists of 1861, would fight a "foreign" invader in order both to defend their homeland and to preserve white-on-top race relationships. Southerners had a not-so-secret weapon: northern democracy. Graybacks could surely endure until their battlefield victories, or, at worst, stalemates, fed home-front dissent and outright disloyalty in Lincolnland. Foreign recognition or aid to the Confederacy seemed likely. Combined, these forces would unleash unstoppable pressures for a negotiated peace, especially at election times (an idea behind the South's 1862 and 1863 thrusts into Maryland and Pennsylvania preceding elections there). Hawkish Southern prophets envisioned peace treaties that included permanent protections for slavery and extradition-like fugitive-recapture clauses.

Southerners misjudged much about the society they had left. Reversing history, the majority of nonseceded America did regain faith in its elected leadership, from Lincoln down. This unanticipated revival of faith proved to be the ultimate misjudgment by the South, one that basically affected the Civil War's pace, nature, and outcome. Fundamentally, this misjudgment centered on the ability of the Union's civilian and military leaders to learn quickly from crises. Confederate makeweights failed to anticipate that their Union counterparts could arm themselves quickly with sound perceptions about the elastic limits of government in domestic crises, perceptions derived from the nation's constitutional history and law. And Southern analysts misread the capacity of the nation's leaders and general population, so armed, not only to hold to the war aim of 1861, but to advance to others such as emancipation. The South failed especially to anticipate Lincoln's educability and character, not to mention the possibility that Northerners might, like their Southern countrymen, also be willing to endure the costs of war.

Northerners also misjudged. Their basic misperception concerned the degree of devotion that even antisecession, nonslaveholder Southerners felt for their static, racially hierarchic society. But because free America was not pinned to rigid racial or constitutional visions, but instead felt served by an adaptable Constitution and educable leaders such as Lincoln, Northerners proved to be able to discard their false or irrelevant misjudgments. Two-party politics, so despised in the South, became the major vehicle for educating the Union public about military and constitutional strategies, and about the risks and hazards attending the abolition of slavery, especially if schemes to colonize freedmen abroad proved to be unworkable, as they eventually did.

These sectional differences became important as the Civil War escalated from the ninety-day militia muster that both Lincoln and Davis initially expected to be the full extent of the war. One year later, the Union — which in 1861 could not stop first seven states, then eleven, from seceding, or protect a single fort — was maneuvering Napoleonic-scale forces against equally huge Confederate armies across a vast arc from northern Virginia to southeast Texas, and southward to the Gulf of Mexico, where the South's major city, New Orleans, fell to Union troops. Warships contested oceanic trade routes while armies and shallow-draft fleets tried to dominate railroad and river systems that allowed strategic mobility and fed the economy. Despite terrible combat casualties in vast stalemate battles, Lincoln, in the midst of 1862's scheduled congressional and state elections, dared to proclaim the emancipation of slaves in still-disloyal states. In 1863, once-lockjawed federal power was conquering Vicksburg and stopping Lee at Gettysburg, reconstructing the governments of whole states and innumerable localities, and recruiting and conscripting whites and blacks (the latter being mostly runaways from slavery) into bluecoated ranks. In 1864, for the first time in the world's history, a warring nation — especially one fighting a civil war — conducted nationwide calendared elections (which Lincoln expected to lose) for a head of government and the majority of legislators, elections in which soldiers voted if their states allowed the practice. Odds are that a negotiated peace involving permanence for the Confederacy and for slavery — the unchanged Confederate war aims since 1861 — would have followed Lincoln's defeat in 1864. By the time Lee surrendered at Appomattox in April 1865, four years after the war began, Union armies had rolled back both secession and slavery to vanishing points.

From Sumter to Appomattox, however, this costly progress was reversible not only by Confederate defenders but also by Northern voters and pro-Southern activists — all of which suggests that the idea of a successful Confederate rebellion was not foolish. Indeed, the abolitionist radical-Republican vision that Lincoln finally accepted — of Bluecoats crushing both secession and slavery, and of the reconquered states raising their internal governing standards to higher levels of popular participation — long seemed the greater foolishness.

This phenomenon of Union adaptability is the more remarkable in that its government and the Confederacy's were so similar in form. Both were organized federally by written constitutions that more or less precisely assigned certain functions to their respective nations, reserved others to member states, left others for either nation or states to perform, and ignored still others. The two national governments, like those of almost every one of the states, were composed of the familiar three branches — the legislative, executive, and judicial. In both the states qualified national as well as state voters, an additional reflection of the incurable state-centeredness prevailing everywhere in America. Both were political democracies, a condition Secessia defined in white-only and partyless terms.

As for war emergency home-front policies, from first to last both the Union and Confederate national and state governments intruded in seemingly similar ways into formerly untouched and untouchable areas of life. Under delegated commander-in-chief authority, soldiers arrested, tried, and imprisoned allegedly or actually disloyal civilians. Northern Democrats decried the growth of "American Bastilles" and denounced "King Linkum I," especially after the president accepted emancipation as a new Union war aim. Important twentieth-century scholars, reacting to emergency policies of their own time, echoed these criticisms of Lincoln (though rarely of Davis) when describing him as a "constitutional dictator."

Yet Davis also ordered soldiers to arrest civilians. Confederate as well as Union congresses and state legislatures imposed loyalty oaths on officials, then on ever-increasing categories of civilians, including lawyers, teachers, travelers, and contractors (though never, in the South, on slaves or free blacks), and censored newspapers — even, in rare instances, temporarily suspending publication. Both warring sections resorted for the first time in American history to conscription (though as late as 1865 the Confederacy refused seriously to consider the drafting or arming of free or slave blacks). Both sides licensed coastal trade, blockaded their own ports, printed paper money, and taxed many consumer goods and individuals' incomes; both, possessing what appeared to be essentially similar *forms* of government, when faced with a long, searing civil war, apparently resorted to similar policies.

But the appearance of similarity is deceptive. For, as suggested earlier, even during this long, searing civil war the Union maintained its capacity to grow, to change, to risk even biracial coexistence on terms other than master-slave. By contrast, the Confederacy held statically to its war aim of 1861. This rigidity helped to lead not only to the military verdict of Appomattox but also to constitutional verdicts against slavery and race-based inequalities in the laws of nation and states.

Over a century later, after much experience with and study of wars of many sorts, including civil wars, we recognize how dynamic they can be. Wars, we understand, can start from certain causes, develop derivative yet differing aims, and then lead to still more differing yet still derivative results. Ralph Waldo Emerson called the Civil War a "dynamometer," and "a new glass to see all our old things through." Well and good for the Union that a leading intellectual like Emerson should so advise his audience. But perhaps it was more important that Lincoln, who made a nation his attentive audience, should rediscover in America's Constitution and history adequate supports for rugged wartime policies; that an obscure Ohio "war" Democrat and Union army officer, Durbin Ward, and many more like him, could grow with Lincoln from the reunion-only war aim of 1861 to one of reunion plus abolition in 1865. In short, the war experience taught a generation that the Constitution was not merely a network of negatives.

In essential ways the North was able better than the South to respond to the war's superheated pressures, in part by reason of this widespread attitude about the Constitution as a flexible source of authority as well as restraints. Southern constitutionalists, political leaders, and voters proved to be committed to the static constitutional ideas that in 1860 and 1861 had justified secession. Therefore, in 1865 as in 1861 the South's war aim was white superiority enshrined in constitutions, laws, and customs. Southern politicians from Jefferson Davis down shared this comforting simplicity of policy position, and many expressed pleasure at the absence of political parties in their states. Secessia's politicians also did not enjoy the benefits offered by fund-raising, patronage-dispensing, criticism-blunting, public-educating, government-lubricating, and policy-formulating services that parties provided in the North. Basic policy alternatives such as arming slaves or seeking reunion could rarely become public questions. Less fundamental changes had few coattails to cling to. In the South, as a result, accountability, responsivity, and adaptation were improbable no matter how desirable or necessary.

Contrast what did not occur in the policy-immobile South with what did take place northward. There, Republicans and "war" Democrats formed coalitions that ultimately sustained Lincoln's antidisloyalty policies, diplomacy, emancipation, conscription, paper-money issues, and wartime reconstructions of occupied rebel states. Congressmen and president approved also monumental so-called nonwar laws (none of which could mean much unless the Bluecoats won). These improved the banking system and lower federal courts, encouraged "homesteaders" to purchase public land cheaply and to establish tax-supported territorial and state universities, and supported private-sector construction of transcontinental railroads. The Congress modernized its internal operations, with the Speaker of the House improving his control over legislative traffic, especially money appropriations. Determined to oversee the swelling numbers of military officers, Congress created the world's first military postal service and America's first joint standing committee, on the Conduct of the War. Commander-in-chief Lincoln quickly established strong, friendly, and intimate links to the committee. It whipsawed upstart generals when he wished not to do so publicly. For its part, the committee monitored war contracts, spoke loudly in matters of military commissions, and increased the president's accountability for all war matters, including the fates of allegedly disloyal civilians who were under arrest and of freed slaves. Which is to say that traditional logrolling, pork-barrel political-party operations adapted quickly to the war's hectic pace and hot issues.

This adaptation was possible because Northern party organizations linked Washington to every state and locality. Some states' legislatures, like the Congress, enacted "war" measures (including test oath laws especially for licensed professionals), created home-guard military units, and set price limits on staple foodstuffs. And, again like the Congress, almost every Union state reformed itself in "nonwar" terms during the Civil War decade, rectifying inequitable gerrymandered election districts, equalizing tax burdens, democratizing voting qualifications, and eradicating old antiblack clauses from the laws. Further, states and localities established numerous new institutions, ranging from city police, fire, and health departments to state and local boards of public education. In the South, however, to state the matter briefly, neither the Confederate national nor state governments risked what latter-day scholars have described as "modernization."

The diverse populations of the reformed Union states re-elected Lincoln and his party colleagues in 1864, ratified the Thirteenth Amendment a year later, and tried through the rest of the 1860s to convince the defeated Confederates to raise their states' standards to similarly improved levels. That the effort became frustrated and derailed by Southerners' continuing devotion to their race advantages suggests that a century ago the surface similarities of the "two governments" were deeply modified by these underlying factors. The Union reached Appomattox greatly changed from the society that in 1861 had learned the news of Fort Sumter's surrender; the Confederacy reached Appomattox in part because of its determination to remain as unchanged as possible from the society that four years earlier had launched the experiment in rebellion.

It seemed incomprehensible to Americans then and later that the people of North and South, brothers, Americans all, could come to blows. Fort Sumter changed that. As the new Rebel banner flew over the parade ground in F. K. Houston's April 15, 1861, image, there literally were two nations out of one. (USAMHI)

But there was a mighty remnant of the old Union behind him as he took his oath of office: the still unfinished Capitol. This image of the ceremonies was taken by a captain of engineers, Montgomery C. Meigs, who was in charge of the Capitol expansion. Soon he would be quartermaster general of Lincoln's armies. (LC)

At first there were substantial doubts about the ability of the untested new president Lincoln to cope with the crisis — to prevent actual war, much less reunite the divided sections. In Alexander Gardner's February 24, 1861, portrait, all of Lincoln's abilities and future promise remain yet untested. (LO)

Top right: A host of diverse — often discordant — elements were what Lincoln had to use to forge a weapon for victory. Within his own party he had to contend with radicals like Thaddeus Stevens of Pennsylvania, men who took a hard-line stance against the South and pushed for immediate progress on emancipation. (LC)

Bottom left: Leading radical Charles Sumner refused even to consider compromise short of reunification and emancipation. Such doctrinaire elements in the president's party were a constant challenge, and sometime embarrassment, to Lincoln. (KA)

Bottom right: Less rigid in their thinking were men like William Seward, Lincoln's secretary of state. Ambitious for the presidency himself, he was at first jealous of the chief executive, even suggesting that Lincoln should let him run the country. (NA)

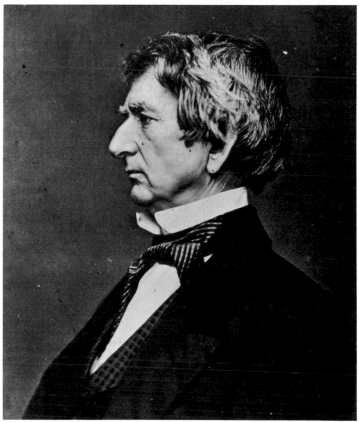

Edwin M. Stanton had been attorney general in Buchanan's Democratic administration. But in 1862, still a Democrat, he became perhaps Lincoln's most effective cabinet minister as secretary of war. (KA)

Lincoln also had to depend upon former Democrats who stood behind the war effort and the cause of the Union. Stephen Douglas, his old political foe from Illinois, campaigned against Lincoln for the presidency in 1860, yet stood squarely behind him for the Union in 1861. (LC)

There was little question that the people of
the Union were behind Lincoln. In the days
after Sumter, scenes like this war rally in
Ann Arbor, Michigan, were repeated all
across the country. (MHC)

And when the first boys went off to war or
returned home — as here, at the return of
the First Michigan to Detroit on August 7,
1861 — the people poured forth their support.
(BHC)

Washington itself was still a city that, like the Union, lay unfinished. Stately
government buildings stood cheek-by-jowl with swamps and shanties. There was still
a sense of uncertainty about where the capital was going as a city and, with its
predominantly Southern heritage, just how loyal it would be to the Union. (USAMHI)

Still there were the symbols of national power, imposing if not quite finished. The Capitol, shown here in April or May of 1865, with Lincoln's mourning crepe still tied to the columns, housed the greatest deliberative body in the hemisphere. Cantankerous, argumentative, occasionally adversarial, the members of Congress were Lincoln's arm's-length allies in the fight for the Union. (NA)

Lincoln's government had a host of weapons
to wage its war, not the least of which was its
economic superiority. The Customs House
in New York City produced enormous
revenue to help finance the war effort, and
in 1863 it did double duty as a branch of the
Treasury. (LC)

The Patent Office, shown in this early prewar
image, was the venter for invention and
enterprise, much of which came to fruition
in the weapons being manufactured for the
Union's armies. (LC)

The North's military and naval might, barely marginal at war's outset, grew to be overwhelming. The Confederacy could never put to sea ships like the mighty *Vandalia*, shown at Portsmouth, New Hampshire, in this 1863 image by H. P. Moore. (JAH)

Indeed, almost from the first Lincoln's navy was able to institute a generally effective blockade of all the major Southern ports. This late-April 1861 image by J. D. Edwards shows the Yankee blockading ships (on the horizon) off Fort Pickens, near Pensacola harbor, literally within days of their arrival. (USAMHI)

In time, Lincoln would also use the cause of the war — slavery — as one of his weapons. Millions of former slaves, like these outside the Hilton Head, South Carolina, plantation home of Brig. Gen. Thomas Drayton of the Confederate army, would flock to the Union's banners. (USAMHI)

The first step was emancipation. Beneath this tree, ever after called Emancipation Oak, a Federal reads to the assembled blacks Lincoln's January 1, 1863, Emancipation Proclamation. By making freedom, at the right time, one of his goals, Lincoln made the fight for the Union a holy crusade. (FL)

That step taken, the next was actually arming blacks to fight for the Union. That same January 1, the First South Carolina Volunteers pose at Port Royal, South Carolina. They are the first unit of former slaves officially enlisted. (LC)

Yet Lincoln had his enemies within his own camp, and the question of loyal opposition versus outright treason became a thorny one. No one epitomized this more than Clement L. Vallandigham of Ohio. Imprisoned by one general for his antiwar speeches, Vallandigham would eventually be banished from the Union briefly, though he was no traitor. (LC)

Especially when they were in Confederate territory, Lincoln's armies had to guard against the disloyal. Loyalty oaths were a commonplace requirement, and many a farmer, like these two in Virginia, was stopped and questioned when suspected of providing aid to the enemy. (HEHL)

Sometimes Northerners took the law into their own hands when dealing with suspected treason. More than one antiwar newspaper suffered the fate of the *Bridgeport* (Connecticut) *Weekly Farmer*, when angry mobs destroyed their presses. Here, on August 24, 1861, furniture and type have been sent crashing through the windows to the streets, and members of the mob still linger. (BPL)

Sometimes unrest broke out in other kinds of civil disturbance, such as the July 1863 draft riots in New York City. Here members of the Seventh New York Militia stand in the city's streets after being called forth to maintain order. (SRF)

What quieted the loyal and disloyal opposition alike in the Union was success. Lincoln's victories came at the right times. Here at Little Round Top at Gettysburg, and elsewhere, his armies won when they had to, sustaining the will of the public to continue the war to victory. (USAMHI)

And thus it was that Washington and that still unfinished Capitol building could host a Grand Review in May 1865 celebrating the victory of the Union. (LC)

Top right: The weapons of war available to the South were far less extensive. Indeed, when South Carolina voted here in Secession Hall to leave the Union in December 1860, there was no government in place as an alternative. (USAMHI)

Bottom left: Everything had to be created for the new Confederacy, from its new president, Jefferson Davis of Mississippi, to the most mundane things, like post office forms. At the inaugural ceremony here in Montgomery, Alabama, on February 18, 1861, the new chief executive . . . (NA)

Bottom right: . . . Jefferson Davis probably did not yet realize fully just how enormous the task ahead of him would be. (NA)

From the outset, the political necessity of having Virginia stand with the South influenced policy, and in the end resulted in the Confederate capital being moved here to Richmond. Politically, the move made sense. Militarily, it put the new capital within 100 miles of Washington, and saddled Davis from the first with a policy that kept Virginia always uppermost in his mind. (LC)

Top right: Davis himself established residence in the old Brockenbrough house, making it the White House of the Confederacy. (USAMHI)

Bottom left: The Confederate House and Senate moved into the old Virginia State House nearby. (USAMHI)

Bottom right: The South did have its share of established governmental systems in place that could be converted to the needs of the new nation, but never nearly enough. The U.S. Customs House in Richmond was symbolic of the financial straits of the Confederacy from the first. Thanks to the blockade, customs duties were only a shadow of what was needed. (LC)

The scarcity of gold and silver made the South's currency wildly inflationary, and her treasuries, like this one in Vicksburg, almost meaningless. Only massive foreign and domestic loans, not real income, kept the government afloat and able to buy the munitions of war. (KA)

Equally chaotic was the banking system, with no national currency other than promissory notes. It was said that a Confederate took his money to market in a wheelbarrow, and brought his purchases home in a pocket. The Bank of Richmond after the surrender. (USAMHI)

Strangely enough, for a region that had
produced so many great statesmen in the
past, the South possessed few of them by
1861 (perhaps one of the reasons that the war
came when it did). Those few, like John
Slidell of Louisiana, were early pressed into
service — Slidell as a diplomat to France. (LC)

Like Lincoln, Davis had to face a considerable
share of opposition in the Confederacy.
There were many like John Minor Botts of
Virginia, seated here among his family, who
would not forswear their loyalty to the old
Union, who withheld their allegiance from
the new Confederacy. Not a few, like Botts,
went to jail for their beliefs. (LC)

More galling to Davis were those so-called fire-eaters who helped bring on secession but who opposed his administration for not being radical enough. Robert Barnwell Rhett of South Carolina was one of their leaders, an almost constant thorn in Davis's side. (LC)

His home, Rhett House, reflected all the values and aspirations that befitted his class, but like so many, Rhett never understood that some of the state rights he loudly championed would have to yield if the Confederacy were to succeed. (USAMHI)

Top right: Davis also faced problems with many of his governors. Both of Virginia's war governors, John Letcher and William Smith, lived here in the governor's mansion and cooperated fully with Davis. (USAMHI)

Bottom left: Others proved more jealous of their prerogatives. Zebulon Vance of North Carolina resisted allowing Tarheel soldiers to be commanded by men from other states, and withheld some supplies and arms that were needed elsewhere in the South. (NCDAH)

Bottom right: Most difficult of all, however, was Georgia governor Joseph Brown. He intentionally withheld Georgia troops from the Confederacy because he refused to acknowledge Richmond's right to command his state's resources. (LC)

Even Davis's own vice-president, frail and diminutive Alexander H. Stephens, opposed him through most of the war, and finally in 1865 simply went home to Georgia well before the collapse of the Confederacy. (LAWLM)

As for Davis, he fought on in spite of all the obstacles before him, becoming at times the personal embodiment of his cause. From the start, he and the Confederacy had faced attempting to do too much with too little. When he was captured May 10, 1865, at Irwinville, Georgia, he was placed in this ambulance and taken back to Macon, with an uncertain future ahead of him and the Confederacy. (LC)

For the men and officers of the fallen South, their armies beaten and crumbling and their government evaporated, there was nothing left but surrender. An unidentified Confederate brigadier meets with Federal general Joseph Hayes in a scene probably posed immediately after Appomattox. (JCF)

They must all, North and South, join hands as, once more, they become what the Union's motto declared, "one out of many." (WAF)

Feeding the Machine

★ ★

Maury Klein

VOLTAIRE once observed that God is always on the side of the biggest battalions. In the American Civil War the world would learn for the first time a whole new definition of biggest battalions. The armies were far larger than anything seen on the continent before and required massive efforts to feed and supply them. North and South alike had not only to produce vast quantities of matériel but also to move them efficiently to the front. To a surprising extent their success or failure in this endeavor shaped the outcome of the war. The North won largely because it had a crushing superiority in resources and created efficient systems for harnessing them; the South lost because it was short of just about everything except courage and never forged systems to utilize effectively the meager resources at its disposal.

It was this new dimension that made the Civil War the first modern war in which numbers, valor, and leadership were no longer enough to assure victory. In the emerging industrial age, the biggest battalions were not at the front but behind the lines: a juggernaut of productivity capable of transforming the face of war itself. From the factories and fields of the North poured forth a seemingly endless flow of food, weapons, ammunition, tools, uniforms, blankets, shoes, wagons, and other supplies. The railroad system moved troops and equipment faster than ever before, while the telegraph moved information even more quickly. Government agencies, swollen in size and number, roused from their slumber of earlier years to grapple with the problems of administering so huge an undertaking. An army might still march on its stomach, but the stomach did not get fed until the paperwork was done.

In this great undertaking the North possessed immense advantages over the South. It had more people and more raw materials, most of the factories, foundries, machinery, tools, railroads, and telegraph lines, as well as the managers, technicians, and skilled workmen to operate them. Unlike the South, the apparatus of government was already in place and manned by experienced bureaucrats. It had ships to import whatever goods or material were needed and a navy to prevent the South from doing the same. Although the South was an agricultural region, the North's farms held an edge in sheer quantity of output and in diversity. Where cotton was king in the South, the North produced vast amounts of wheat, corn, meat, dairy products, and wool to replace the cotton lost from Southern sources.

Under the new conditions of war, these advantages increased over time. The side with the biggest industrial battalions actually grew stronger as the war progressed. What began as a diffuse, fumbling effort to supply the armies evolved gradually into an efficient engine of productivity harnessed to coordinated systems of organization. The North might lose heart or grow discouraged over its appalling losses, but it would never falter for want of the resources to prosecute the war. By 1864 it had become a mighty storehouse of soldiers and supplies against which the Confederacy could not hope to compete on anything like equal terms.

For the South the reverse held true: as the war progressed it grew steadily weaker through an inability to replenish losses of every kind. Lack of factories, mines, and raw materials made its output skimpy from the start and therefore wholly unequal to replacement needs. Machines wore out for want of new parts, and bent or broken tools stayed in service long after they ought to have been retired, because new ones could not be obtained. The Southern railroad system was run into the ground long before enemy troops made "hairpins" out of its worn and overworked rails. Most of the lines would have needed rebuilding after the war even if Yankee marauders had inflicted no damage on them.

Without a transportation system, the South could not move vitally needed supplies from one region to another. Food for the troops was plentiful even in 1865, but no way could be found to get it to the men. Since most of the war was fought on Southern soil, large chunks of the Confederacy were lost to the ravages of battle, conquest, or despoliation. As the South's domain shrank, so did its already feeble store of resources. The naval blockade reduced the flow of imports from abroad to a mere trickle, and the fall of Vicksburg in 1863 all but eliminated the trans-Mississippi West as a source of supplies. Early in the war Southern troops found themselves in the position of guerrilla fighters obliged to live off arms and equipment scavenged from the enemy on the battlefield.

For all its efforts to organize a government capable of prosecuting the war efficiently, the South's mobilization seldom reached beyond the level of improvisation on a grand scale. It lacked the resources, the managerial talent, the organizational skills, and the social or political philosophy to do anything more. A people wedded to state rights and suffused with an exaggerated sense of individualism were not likely candidates for creating a united front. Victory was possible only through cooperation at every level, yet too many Southern leaders preferred defending their principles in rancorous disputes to solving problems through compromise. Often their intransigence defied the bounds of common sense. This divisiveness aggravated the already serious shortages and lack of productivity that plagued the Confederacy.

None of this was apparent in 1861 except to a select few with cool heads and alert eyes. In the first flush of martial enthusiasm that swept North and South alike, it was widely believed that the war would be a brief affair, won or lost on some decisive battlefield by the valor of a few good men. Once the fiasco at Bull Run shattered this illusion, both sides turned in earnest to the task of mobilizing for a war of indeterminate length and unprecedented scale.

Only then did the shocking disparity in resources between the sections become apparent. The most obvious differences lay in sheer numbers. Some 22 million people lived in the North and only 9 million in the South, of whom about 3.5 million were slaves who would be used as labor but not as soldiers. Immigration flowed almost entirely to the North, adding another 800,000 people to that section during the war years alone. The South produced less than 10 percent of the nation's industrial goods and possessed only 8,783 miles of railroad compared to 22,385 miles for the North. Most of the country's coal, iron ore, copper, gold, silver, salt, and that new wonder, petroleum, were found in the North.

Impressive as these numbers were, they only hint at the true dimensions of Northern superiority. That section also contained most of what might be called the infrastructure of industrial productivity: machinery, machine tools, factories, furnaces, forges, foundries, rolling mills, steam engines, technicians, skilled workmen, managers, and inventors. Conversion to war industries came quickly if not always easily. When the flow of Southern cotton to New England slowed, cotton mills and carpet mills became woolen mills. When workmen joined the army, women and children took their places. Machine shops produced guns, saw factories turned out sabers, and jewelry factories made brass buttons. The government armory at Springfield, Massachusetts, employed three thousand men and produced a thousand rifles a day, while private contractors turned out twice that number.

From New England's mills flowed a swelling stream of uniforms, blankets, shoes, and other items. The sewing machine, barely a decade old in 1860, galvanized wartime production. Men's shirts that once required more than fourteen hours to produce by hand could be done in little over an hour. The new McKay sewing machine enabled one person to sew several hundred pairs of shoes a day. Thanks to the war's demands, ready-made clothing exploded into a major industry. New factories sprang up in cities as if by magic. Philadelphia, the manufacturing center of the North, welcomed 180 new establishments between 1862 and 1864. Chicago emerged as "Porkopolis"—the meat-packing capital of America—during these years and could scarcely keep count of the new agricultural-implement factories, carriage and wagon factories, tanneries, machine shops, foundries, breweries, distilleries, and other industries that opened in the city. Even sleepy New Haven saw six large new factories go up in a single year.

Shipyards in Maine, textile mills in Rhode Island, shovel works in Massachusetts, arms factories in Connecticut, iron furnaces in Pennsylvania, rolling mills in Ohio, locomotive plants in New Jersey, wagon works in Indiana — these and countless others poured out goods in amounts that staggered the imagination. "The war," observed a Massachusetts editor in 1863, "has brought into activity many mechanical employments for which there is little occasion in time of peace." Old industries flourished and new ones sprouted. The army's need for food gave rise to the canned-food industry, including Gail Borden's amazing canned milk. Wartime demands called forth new weapons, new products, new machines, new techniques, and a record flow of new ideas. More patents (over five thousand) were issued in 1864 than in any previous year.

Northern agriculture matched the impressive record of Northern industry and drew upon the same sources of inspiration. A land of small farmers might have been crippled by so many thousands of its citizens marching off to war, but production suffered little if at all from their absence. Reliance on machinery helped keep yields high even when labor was scarce. Although mowers and reapers were still fairly new when the war broke out, their use spread rapidly. In 1864 factories churned out more than seventy thousand mowers, twice the number of 1862; that same year, 1864, Cyrus McCormick alone produced six thousand reapers. Cultivators, horse-rakes, new harrows, corn planters, steam threshers, grain drills, and similar devices were also marketed. Like other war contractors, the manufacturers of farm implements smelled bonanza profits in the wind, and they were right. "A hundred thousand agricultural laborers are gone; how are we to meet the deficiency?" asked a Cincinnati editor. "We have met it," he answered, "chiefly by labor-saving machinery."

And by drawing out more labor. Someone had to drive the mowers and reapers and tend to the hundred other chores of raising crops. Like the factories of New England, Northern farms leaned heavily on the women and children left behind. "I saw the wife of one of our parishioners," wrote a missionary in Kansas, "driving the team in a reaper; her husband is at Vicksburg. With what help she can secure and the assistance of her little children, she is carrying on the farm." Another reported from Iowa that he saw "more women driving teams on the road and saw more at work in the fields than men." A popular song urged men to

> Just take your gun and go:
> For Ruth can drive the oxen, John,
> And I can use the hoe!

Through these devices Northern farms managed to produce enough corn, wheat, oats, and meat to feed Union armies and still sell large surpluses to England, which suffered three consecutive years of crop failures. Hog and cattle output jumped sharply in the North and the number of sheep doubled, enabling wool production to soar from 60 million pounds in 1860 to 140 million pounds in 1865. This increase did much to fill the gap left by the loss of Southern cotton, although some mills continued to operate on contraband cotton smuggled north. Whatever the fortunes of war, the breadbasket of the Union never ran empty or even lean.

The South strove desperately to match this harnessing of resources. "Mechanical arts and industrial pursuits hitherto practically unknown to our people are already in operation," proclaimed Alabama governor A. B. Moore in October 1861. "The clink of the hammer and the busy hum of the workshop are beginning to be heard through our land. Our manufactures are rapidly increasing." Certainly there was reason for hope. That same year a survey by *Debow's Review* listed dozens of newly established plants in Southern towns for making guns, uniforms, swords, spurs, canteens, steam engines, tent cloth, textiles, rope, leather, candles, plows, stoves, and other products.

Much of this optimism derived from a few showcase facilities that were developed or enlarged during the war. The crown jewel of Southern industry was the Tredegar Iron Works in Richmond, virtually the only factory in the South capable of turning out locomotives or heavy ordnance. At its peak Tredegar employed twenty-five hundred men and operated subsidiary iron furnaces, coal mines, a tannery, a sawmill, and a brick factory. Tredegar not only supplied the Confederacy with munitions and other matériel but also furnished Southern arsenals with essential equipment for their manufacturing. Together with the government-operated Richmond Armory and Arsenal, Tredegar provided about half the ordnance supplied to Confederate armies.

After 1862 Selma, Alabama, emerged as a major site of wartime industries for the South. Using iron ore and coal from nearby mines and machinery run through the blockade from England, the Selma complex included an arsenal, a naval yard, a naval foundry, and facilities for making powder. A major powder works was erected at Augusta, Georgia, and smaller plants for war implements went up in cities throughout the Southeast. The effort was impressive but wholly inadequate to the needs of Southern armies. A major problem for the Confederacy was not merely developing new industry but also

keeping hold of what they had. Nashville was an important industrial site until Union troops captured it in February 1862. The fall of New Orleans that same year cost the South the resources of that city. Every loss of territory crippled the Confederacy's ability to wage war in some way.

The two words that best characterize the Southern war effort are *shortages* and *substitutes*. The Confederacy was short of nearly everything and scrounged frantically after substitutes for what it did not have. Factories lacked iron, lubricating oils, nails, screws, new parts to replace worn ones, even containers and sacks. When existing supplies were used up, replacements were difficult to find and the army always had first claim on what little was produced. Farms suffered no less than factories from shortages. Draft animals suffered heavier casualties than soldiers and were as hard to replace. Horses or mules gone to war could not pull plows. Basic tools and implements, plows, harnesses, saddles, rope, barrels, tubs, and even such simple items as buckets and troughs wore out, and new ones were difficult if not impossible to obtain.

Nothing hurt Southern productivity more than its chronic shortage of skilled labor. The occupation of mechanic was not an honored one in the South; many of the region's best men were Northerners who went home after the firing on Fort Sumter. Wartime aggravated this shortage by increasing the demands on a limited pool of skilled workers and by reducing that pool even further as workers departed to serve in the military. From Charlotte, North Carolina, came a report in May 1864 that "a number of our most important tools are idle a large portion of the time for want of mechanics to work them, and some of these tools, the steam-hammer for instance, are the only tools of their class in the Confederacy." The *Richmond Enquirer* complained bitterly that shoe production in that city had stopped because "of the absence of the operatives at the front. . . . There is an abundance of leather here, and if the shoemakers were not absent, many thousands of pairs of shoes might now be on hand."

Despite dogged Confederate efforts to patch up old equipment and find substitute materials, both factory and farm productivity dwindled steadily because of shortages. Southern women, too, replaced men called to the front, running plantations or toiling in the fields of smaller farms. Their contributions were heroic but in vain. Lack of labor, tools, and seed, loss of acreage to enemy troops, and even bad weather cut deeply into the region's production of food. Southern fire-eaters who had boasted that cotton was king soon had to eat their words but could not eat the cotton or even sell it once the blockade clamped down. King Cotton changed uniform to King Corn as land was shifted to the planting of provisions, but the switch came too late. By 1864 the South faced the grim and bitter irony of being an agricultural region unable to feed itself, let alone its armies.

From the first, transportation posed a major problem. It was not enough merely to produce the stuff of war. Men, equipment, and supplies had to be sent in vast quantities to the right place at the right time in the right amounts. In the field an army moved not only on its stomach but on its arms and with its wagons, horses, and mules — all of which had to be furnished in great numbers. The scale of war in the industrial age transformed logistical problems into nightmares of complexity that demanded fresh approaches to old problems.

Two technological marvels were at the disposal of both sides: the railroad and the telegraph. Here, too, the North had an overwhelming advantage. Apart from possessing most of the nation's railroad track and telegraph lines, it had the men, the matériel, and the technical expertise to keep both in superb condition throughout the war. Where the South had a collection of railroads, the North had what could reasonably be called a rail system linking all of its major cities and water outlets. Northern rivers extended the utility of the region's railroads; Southern rivers acted as little more than obstacles to rail lines.

Southern lines, built largely to accommodate the cotton trade, tended to run "nowhere except from the fields to the sea." Rival cities vying for trade supremacy discouraged connections between the railroads reaching them. Whole sections of the Confederacy lacked any sort of decent rail connection. Moreover, the main routes across the seaboard and from the Ohio-Mississippi valley to the seaboard were roundabout lines

interrupted by repeated transfers. By contrast Northern rails snaked into every major corner of the region and connected with one another to provide an uninterrupted flow of traffic. Northern railroads were better built, possessed better facilities, and had superior equipment in every respect than Southern ones. The four eastern trunk lines alone had as much rolling stock as all the railroads in Dixie.

After a slow start caused by the venal and shortsighted policies of Secretary of War Simon Cameron, the North utilized its rail superiority with devastating effect. The ability to move troops and supplies rapidly by train all but neutralized the South's geographical advantage of possessing the interior line. As Union armies penetrated deeper into the Confederacy, the use of railroads kept their supply lines open and flowing freely. A talented engineer named Herman Haupt developed techniques of bridge building that replaced burned or missing spans so quickly that one astonished onlooker cried, "The Yankees can build bridges faster than the Rebs can burn them down." Alongside the track a string of poles carried telegraph wires that kept the line of communications open wherever the armies went. Only Sherman, on his march to the sea, found himself unable to wire headquarters.

By contrast the Southern railroads, the lifelines of its war effort, wore down like a game but overmatched boxer. The soft iron rails of that era needed constant replacement; so did ties made of wood that the climate attacked voraciously. New engines or cars, parts or tools for maintenance, grew difficult and then impossible to procure. Unlike their enemy, the Confederates lacked the tools, talent, and technique for repairing damage wrought by Union raiders or advancing armies. The North, it seemed, could not only build railroads faster but also tear them up far more effectively than the South. The Southern army could scavenge weapons from the battlefield but not locomotives or boxcars from a roundhouse or depot.

As the Confederate transportation system staggered and faltered before its final collapse, Southern cities and whole regions suffered severe privation and faced the real threat of starvation. By 1865 the South had been stripped of so much of its wherewithal for war that it was surviving on raw courage alone. Phil Sheridan's devastation of the Shenandoah Valley cost the Confederacy a major breadbasket at a time when it lacked the means to ship food in quantity any distance. The bitter defense of Richmond had less to do with saving the capital than with preserving Tredegar and the last major railhead left to the South. Without Tredegar and some semblance of a rail line, the South could not hope to prolong the fight. In those final weeks Robert E. Lee's army starved and shivered in rags while huge caches of food, forage, and clothing waited for them in the distance.

For a century Americans have with fine impartiality fought and refought the bloody battles of the Civil War, relishing their every detail, savoring the valor of brave men and the ignominy of incompetents or cowards. In the end, however, victory came for reasons that had little to do with glory or valor. The North won a war of attrition. There was nothing noble or glamorous about it, and precious little that could be passed down as the stirring tales and great deeds of heroes. But that was the way with this new version of the biggest battalions, in which clerks and quartermasters, engineers and mechanics, managers and bureaucrats fought in their own manner as hard as soldiers. They did not wear uniforms or march to the martial airs of bands or gather around campfires or thrill to the smoke and din of battle. All they did was win.

Top left: Poor as the South was in industry at war's outset, that condition was made even worse by the fact that so much of the region's industrial capacity was concentrated in relatively few areas—particularly Richmond, Virginia. Manchester, across the James River from Richmond, boasted several factories. (LC)

Top right: Like Haxall & Crenshaw's establishment, they were chiefly flour mills, dependent upon the river both for water power and for transportation of raw materials via the James River Canal. One of its locks is just visible in the foreground. (LC)

For shipping itself, whether in peace or wartime, the South was also ill prepared, with only a handful of shipyards—such as the one here, also in Richmond. Philadelphia photographers Levy & Cohen made this image in April 1865, showing two canal boats still under construction. (LCP)

The Virginia State Arsenal, in ruins in this 1865 image, also made Richmond a center of Confederate arms manufacture, . . . (LC)

. . . just as the Tredegar Iron Works, the Confederacy's only major foundry capable of casting cannons and ship's armor, helped make the city an object of Federal desire. Capturing Richmond would put an end to a major share of the South's industrial war effort. (VM)

From the arsenal and Tredegar poured a steady stream of guns, solid shot, shell, ordnance, and ammunition of every description. (LC)

Manufacture for the Confederate armies did
take place elsewhere, thanks in large part
to the ingenuity of men like Col. George
Washington Rains. It was he who designed
and operated . . . (ARCM)

. . . the Augusta (Georgia) Powder Works.
Despite hardship and shortage, its output of
high-grade powder for Rebel armies was
prodigious, a credit to what hard work and
innovation could accomplish. (LC)

But some of the South's manufacturing was scattered in little cities and towns like
Macon, Georgia, far enough from danger to protect it from strong Federal threat,
but at the same time too small in output to be really significant in meeting
Confederate needs. (GDAH)

Schofield's Iron Works in Macon was just two years old when war broke out. (HP)

Still, its small steam engine . . . (HP)

. . . and its larger one were turned to Rebel ordnance needs when the fighting came. (HP)

Beyond the heavy manufacturing, much of what was produced in the South came from the hands of its women, whose fingers and needles had to provide the clothing, flags, and bandages that the factories could not, and whose labor had to till the fields of the men who were away in uniform. A Timothy O'Sullivan image of Southern women on the Cedar Mountain, Virginia, battlefield in 1862. (LC)

The South was still a horse-and-buggy region — or, as here, an ox-and-cart one. Cameramen Armistead & White of Corinth, Mississippi, photographed this Southern civilian hauling slab wood in Federally occupied Corinth. (CHS)

It was an even greater misfortune for the Confederacy that so much of its industrial capability lay directly in the path of the Yankee armies. Southern railroads, inferior in quality and mileage at the outset, suffered further setbacks with the fall of Nashville. The Chattanooga depot appears in the foreground, with the Tennessee State House in the distance. (LC)

An even greater blow came with the fall of Atlanta, the Confederacy's major rail interchange. Here George Barnard photographed the ruins of the roundhouse used by the Georgia Railroad and by the Atlanta & West Point Railroad. The loss of its already worn rolling stock, and the cutting of its rail lines, made it increasingly impossible for the South to get its meager produce and manufactures to the armies that needed them. (NA)

This tiny little four-wheeled fire engine, photographed in Richmond at war's end, almost symbolizes the crushing inability of the Confederacy's resources to extinguish the Northern conflagration that ravaged the South. (LC)

By contrast, even though unprepared for war when it came, the North had all the pieces in place to wage a victorious effort. Its factories were spread all over the nation, as here at the Harpers Ferry Armory, just across the river at right. (LC)

The oil to lubricate Northern machinery was coming out of the ground in Pennsylvania, with a whole new industry burgeoning just as the war commenced. (DWM)

New fortunes were about to be made, even as the Union was caught up in the
greatest test it ever faced. (DWM)

And to keep the furnaces supplied with iron ore, mines from Michigan to New England poured forth a constant flow of mineral. Out of earth like this in the Jackson Mine in northern Michigan came rifles and buttons, cannons, stirrups, and every manner of hardware that mind could conceive or soldier could need. (MDSSA)

At first, though, even the best Yankee potential was no better than the men responsible for directing the war effort, and Simon Cameron of Pennsylvania, Lincoln's first secretary of war, was not the man for the job. Only with his departure did the mobilizing and marshaling of the Northern resources and organization begin to tell. (USAMHI)

In communications, so vital in this first really mobile and virtually continental war, Washington enjoyed preeminence from the outset. From Signal Corps headquarters here in Washington, and from several other places, a constant flow of information was available daily from the far-flung Union armies. (USAMHI)

Some of that information was gathered right at the front by men atop signal observation towers like this one on Cobb's Hill on the Appomattox River, outside Petersburg. (USAMHI)

The information, once collected, was sped back to the rear, no matter where the Yankee armies went, thanks to the work of the Military Telegraph Corps. Many of its men and wagons pose here outside Richmond in June 1865, their task finished. (USAMHI)

They established their camps right at the front and stayed with the armies. Most of the time telegraphers like these at Bealton, Virginia, in August 1863, had more to do than lounge and feast. (USAMHI)

Their lines stretched everywhere. Here the wire comes down out of the wood at the right, near Lookout Mountain, not far from Chattanooga. (USAMHI)

In Virginia, where the wire is supported by a hastily erected pole, staff officers gather at a church to discuss the latest information. (USAMHI)

The Union stood just as unchallenged in its transportation capabilities. The great roundhouse and depot at Alexandria, Virginia, across the Potomac from Washington, was one of scores of major rail installations. In this image by Capt. A. J. Russell, the Union's only official army photographer, hundreds of soldiers stand in the distance, perhaps awaiting transportation, while rolling stock and firewood everywhere attest to the Union's rail strength. (USAMHI)

Even when the Confederates managed to
reach and tear up sections of Yankee track,
the interruptions in rail traffic were brief.
Here workers repair a part of the Orange &
Alexandria Railroad near Catlett's Station,
Virginia. (USAMHI)

Ingenious railroadmen devised speedy ways
to restore damaged track, like this brace
supporting a broken rail. It was much quicker
than laying new track. (NA)

The tracks were a lifeline for the Union war effort, and nothing received greater care and tending. (USAMHI)

New rolling stock and engines moved from the Atlantic to the Mississippi — among them this engine, a tribute to Gen. Herman Haupt, chief of construction of the U.S. Military Railroad, the man responsible for many of the wonders achieved. (USAMHI)

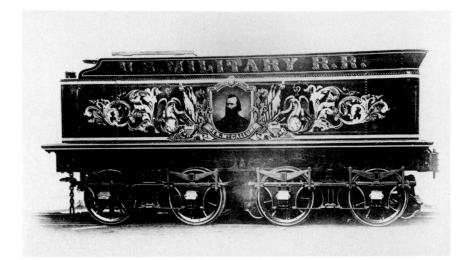

Honored, too, was Col. Daniel C. McCallum, director of the Union's military railroads. Despite this tender's illustration, McCallum's rank as a general was only informal. (USAMHI)

As they moved into Confederate territory, McCallum's and Haupt's legions quickly appropriated remaining Rebel rails. J. D. Heywood, photographer of New Bern, made this image of a "conductor's car" on the nearby Atlantic & North Carolina Railroad. But it was an engine of the United States Military Railroad that pulled it now. (USAMHI)

The feats Haupt's bridge builders could achieve staggered the imagination. Here at Chattanooga, the conquering Federals had found only the remaining stone piers of a burned bridge across the Tennessee River. The men who lived in the camp in the foreground rebuilt it in record time. (USAMHI)

They could build a simple trestle to carry newly laid line across a gully. (USAMHI)

Or they could rebuild a destroyed six-hundred-foot bridge, like this one over the Etowah in Georgia constructed during Sherman's Atlanta campaign. (USAMHI)

The story was the same with shipping. Wherever Lincoln's armies went, they commanded the rivers and the seas, and used them to keep a steady flow of supplies coming to Union quartermasters. Supply bases like this one at White House Landing on Virginia's Pamunkey River sprouted the moment soldier and sailor could forge a link between each other. (USAMHI)

Once forged, that link was strengthened with unending traffic. Here the Pamunkey teems with supply and transport vessels in 1864. (USAMHI)

The year before, the Army of the Potomac's supply base had been here at Aquia Creek Landing, where every kind of vessel was pressed into service, from tugboats to scows to river packets. (USAMHI)

Steam vessels augmented with sails even plied the rivers. (USAMHI)

Whatever their source of power, the ships brought with them an endless line of barges and other small craft, each one crammed with munitions or food, or both. Here the James River in 1864 teems with traffic of every description. At far right, the captured Confederate ironclad *Atlanta,* with its distinctive sloping sides, patrols the stream. (USAMHI)

Sailing vessels like these schooners even helped when at anchor—as here, where they provide stability for a long pontoon bridge over the James at Weyanoke Point. (USAMHI)

Powering most of these Yankee ships was coal, consumed in unfathomable quantities, and shipped to several major supply bases like the government coal wharf here at Alexandria. The produce of Pennsylvania's coalfields sent warships and supplies everywhere that water could take them. (USAMHI)

The men themselves, soldiers numbering in the tens of thousands, went to war aboard great transports like the *Thorne* (at left) and the *Prometheus*, photographed here on June 28, 1864. (USAMHI)

Here in the same slip, on June 16, had berthed *El Cid*. In the constant traffic, ships did not stay put for long. (USAMHI)

The greatest water-fed supply base of all, however, was Grant's at City Point, so vital in his months-long siege of Petersburg. More men, matériel, munitions, and foodstuffs passed through here than through any previous supply base in military history. (USAMHI)

Responsible for getting the right things to the right people at the right place were the army quartermasters, based in Washington, with offices spread all over the country, as here in Alexandria. (USAMHI)

From those main offices, the supplies went to the quartermaster's offices with the armies. The quartermaster's department of the Army of the Potomac at Aquia Creek Landing, shown here in February 1863, controlled the flow of matériel to Gen. Joseph Hooker as he prepared for his Chancellorsville campaign in May. (USAMHI)

The quartermasters could build virtual mountains. Commissary wagons of the Federal V Corps receive boxes and barrels of bread and pickled meat brought to them by rail from the supply base. (LC)

Emptied of their loads, the boxcars and flatcars returned to the base for another burden in a ceaseless dance between supply base and soldiers. (USAMHI)

At bases like City Point there was little or no sleep, it seemed. The ships and trains, wagons, boxcars, barrels, and crates moved night and day. In July 1864, when this image was made, Grant was just beginning the enormous buildup that would choke Petersburg in a ten-month siege. (USAMHI)

Any building with sufficient space to be useful was pressed into service to house commissary stores, like this one at Aiken's Landing on the James, shown in January 1865. (USAMHI)

Responsible for ensuring that the system ran smoothly within each army was the office of the assistant quartermaster. Hooker's appears here at Fairfax Court House, Virginia, in June 1863. (USAMHI)

The supplies flowed from that office to a host of smaller depots. The artillery brigade of the VI Corps, Army of the Potomac, had its own commissary storehouse. (USAMHI)

Beef cattle moved in herds wherever the men went, and if men went where animals could not follow, the beeves were slaughtered and their meat "pickled" and packed in barrels for shipment. The process had its flaws, leading the soldiers to refer to the smelly stuff in the barrels as "blue beef." (USAMHI)

There were commissary depots out in Georgia
with Sherman, on Rocky Face Ridge. (USAMHI)

And there were more lush commissary offices
on Hilton Head Island, South Carolina,
shown here in September 1864 by the camera
of Samuel Cooley. (USAMHI)

There was a modest, tented depot at Stoneman's Station, in Virginia . . . (USAMHI)

. . . and a major base at Brandy Station near the Rappahannock, photographed in 1863 by the Bostwick Brothers. (VM)

Wherever the supply bases and commissary depots were located, they all led to this: the butchers cutting the meat and soldiers doling out the bread and rations to the men in the field. Considering its time and place, the whole system worked magnificently, playing no small part in the defeat of the Confederacy. A commissary depot with the Army of the Potomac in April 1864. (LC)

Whatever could be used to help win a war, the Yankee warmakers in Washington shipped to their armies. A. J. Russell's image of the City Point depot and quartermaster's buildings barely hints at the variety. (USAMHI)

Ordnance storehouses and armorer's shops like these on Hilton Head supplied and maintained the cannons that reduced Rebel forts into submission. (USAMHI)

Ordnance yards like this one on Hilton Head stored uncountable cannons and carriages, parts of guns, ammunition, and more. (USAMHI)

Samuel Cooley's camera caught much of the picture of Union might on Hilton Head, not by photographing Yankee soldiers, but by focusing upon what was sent for them to use. (USAMHI)

Lincoln's cavalrymen were supplied the best horses that his Cavalry Bureau could find as it tread a difficult path between dishonest contractors who sold unsound mounts and corrupt officials in the bureau itself who tried to profit at the troopers' expense. These government stables in Chattanooga gave the Union's steeds the best care that horses at war could hope to receive. (USAMHI)

Here at Giesboro Point on the Potomac, with Washington in the background, stood the largest cavalry depot in the nation. (USAMHI)

Its stables sent thousands of mounts out to the cavalrymen in the field. (USAMHI)

A modern army had to be able to maintain itself when it put into the field, and the ever-industrious Yankees brought their own forges and repair facilities with them, as here at City Point. (USAMHI)

These mechanics attached to the First Division of the IX Corps were prepared to repair whatever needed mending. (USAMHI)

Mostly they worked to keep the army vehicles rolling. At government repair shops like these on the Franklin Pike, outside Nashville, worn-out wagons, broken wheels, and more awaited their turn under the hammers of men who forged victory with tools other than rifle and bayonet. (USAMHI)

Yankee ingenuity extended even to "making" water. Here at Beaufort, South Carolina, a saltwater condenser next to the coal dock separated salt from seawater. The result was relatively pure water, and salt vital for preserving meat. (USAMHI)

Lincoln's soldiers could build whatever they needed, when and where they needed
it. When they required a hospital, they built one, like this mammoth general hospital
going up near Bermuda Hundred, Virginia, in 1864. (USAMHI)

As many amenities of home life as possible were provided. Mail from loved ones, so important in maintaining morale, came right to the front, thanks to the military post office. This outpost at Brandy Station, Virginia, photographed in April 1864, often could have a letter in a soldier's hands less than a week after it was mailed from home. (USAMHI)

The men who kept the armies going worked out of tents and sheds when they had to, and occupied better quarters when they could. No sooner did Confederates evacuate a city or town than the bureaus that supplied the Yankee armies moved in. The post office in Petersburg was quickly turned into a quartermaster's office within days after Lee's army departed. The Union juggernaut, so well fed, so well prepared, so well supplied, seemed unstoppable. (USAMHI)

For the Confederacy, alas, it was nothing but the opposite — as symbolized so well by this modest little place, Appomattox Station, Virginia. Lee and his army, abandoning Petersburg, desperately needed more supplies if they were to have a hope of continuing in the field. They were to find them here. But Union interference, dilapidated Rebel railroads, and shortages in supplies all conspired against Lee. When he reached this place, there was nothing awaiting him. The general still had an army, but with nothing left to feed that once magnificent machine, there was no place it could go, nothing it could do. (LC)

Camp Nelson

Mr. Lincoln's Microcosm

A portfolio of a Yankee installation in occupied
Kentucky that reflected the myriad undertakings that
kept the Union armies ascendant in the field

Boone's Knob on the Kentucky River overlooked parts of the area that Lincoln's soldiers turned into only one of scores of behind-the-lines installations designed to sustain the war effort; hold, occupy, and maintain the peace in a portion of the reclaimed South; and exist as much by self-sustenance as possible. (NA)

It was a scenic area, far removed from the war front, and virtually unvisited by the conflict after 1862. The anonymous photographer who made these images could indulge himself in a bit of scenery like the Hickman Bridge over the Kentucky not far from Camp Nelson. (NA)

But it was the camp itself that attracted his chief interest. For the officers in command, the post headquarters was a far cry from the kinds of headquarters inhabited by most of the generals in the field. Grant and Lee lived most of the war in tents. The commander here had a roof—and a cupola—over his head, porches for the sultry summer evenings, and a small pond surrounded by a white gravel walk. (NA)

Top left: There was always fresh water, thanks to the nearby Kentucky. Water pipes ran up the bluff from the river. (NA)

Top right: Steam-powered pumps in the engine house sent tons of water up the steep hillside to . . . (NA)

. . . the camp reservoir on top. (NA)

The water was aerated in a primitive way, and officers could enjoy the view from the little gazebo inside the reservoir's picket-fence enclosure. (NA)

Not far away stood the Ordnance Office, constant reminder that this peaceful post was a part of a war. (NA)

If that were not enough, the array of cannons at the Ordnance Depot recalled well enough why everyone was here. Yet it is an odd mix of pieces in the yard—a couple of napoleons, a couple of ordnance rifles, and, second from the left, an old prewar smoothbore gun with handles, probably a veteran of the Mexican War. Equipping Camp Nelson with the most up-to-date ordnance was obviously not a high priority. (NA)

But regardless of the vintage of its artillery, the guns had to have ammunition, and that called for a magazine for safe storage of powder and shell. Few field installations could boast of so fine a magazine, complete with wooden conduits emerging from the earth to provide interior ventilation. (NA)

Armaments were incidental to Camp Nelson's greater purpose: construction and maintenance of the vehicles that were so vital to the armies. The engineers required lived in these quarters. (NA)

And these are the shops where the engineers and mechanics worked. Every imaginable sort of activity is going on here. Planking for the wagons abounds. Iron stock, either for hoops for the wagon tops or perhaps to be turned into wheel "tires," stands stacked in abundance. (NA)

Farriers bend over horses' hooves; black-smiths toil at anvils, shaping the shoes. (NA)

Horses awaiting their turn stand before the workshops. (NA)

Nearby, the forage shops collected and prepared the grain and grass necessary to feed the hundreds of animals necessary for the camp's officers and vehicles. (NA)

The blacksmiths' shop did what was needed to bend iron to the needs of men. Everything of metal required to build one of the ambulances at left could be produced in this shop. (NA)

Not far away, the carpenters' shop could do the same for the wooden needs of wagons and soldiers alike. Its artisans pose proudly with the tools of their trade. (NA)

The carpenters could do what they did at Camp Nelson thanks largely to having their own steam-powered sawmill, which helped turn hundreds of trees into wagon boxes, carriage wheels, barracks, and more. (NA)

The machine shop, also steam-powered, could further refine the mill's raw planks, or machine with more precision the smithy's forged iron. (NA)

The wagon yard, not far off, was where the newly built or repaired vehicles were assembled and stored. (NA)

The ambulance yard was kept separate, with the ambulances parked in rows, some of them not yet finished. (NA)

The inspection yard stood near some earthworks that never had to hear the sound of battle. Here government inspectors examined the horses being purchased by agents for use as cavalry mounts. (NA)

Those that passed the inspection, along with the hundreds of mules purchased for wagon teams, were penned here before shoeing and training. (NA)

Their next stop was the mule chute. Its crude but effective apparatus was designed to keep a mule upright and off its feet so that all four hooves could be shod at once, reducing the time required for the operation by almost three-fourths. (NA)

All those animals required stables. The officers had a stable all their own for their mounts. (NA)

The enlisted men in the cavalry units garrisoned in or near the camp had their own separate stables. Cavalry mounts with the armies in the field enjoyed nothing at all like this luxury. (NA)

Grain sheds kept stored in the proper conditions the tons of sacked oats and corn needed to sustain the animals. (NA)

The sides of the large shed at center almost seem to bulge outward from its heavy burden, and it does appear that a good bit of grain lies scattered about the yard outside. (NA)

Of course, Camp Nelson had to have a garrison. Units varied through the war but, appropriately enough in this conflict, some of the soldiers were black troops, such as those shown here before their barracks. (NA)

Having a garrison required all of the usual support services beyond the special functions being served at Camp Nelson. The office of the quartermaster and commissary saw to it that the men were fed and clothed. The canvas hoses in the wagon in the foreground suggest that protection against fire was another concern. (NA)

"Q.M. Stores Warehouse No. 1," in the foreground, and its nearby counterparts saw a constant traffic of supplies coming in and going out. (NA)

The men had to eat from those stores, and that called for mess houses like these used by civilian employees and artisans working in the camp. (NA)

No army could get by without bread. Camp Nelson made its own in the "U.S. Bakery," where the empty barrels at left attested to the quantity of flour and other ingredients used. (NA)

Since everywhere that men gathered in large numbers there were bound to be the unruly, a provost marshal's office was needed. It stands at left, and to the right, more sinister, stands the stockade for those who stepped beyond the military law. (NA)

Inside that stockade stood the military prison—sturdily built, with as few windows as possible and surrounded by guard towers at every corner of the palisade. Alas, not every Billy Yank was a hero. (NA)

And wherever the armies went, sickness and disease followed. It was an age ignorant of sanitation, an age when men had never been exposed to large groups of people before. Camp Nelson's convalescent camp was a small city of tents filled with men on the mend. (NA)

The more serious cases, including those with wounds from some of the western battlefields, inhabited the sturdier confines of the general hospital. (NA)

A special section was designated the "Eruptive Hospital," for those suffering with rashes and other skin maladies. (NA)

And for those whose active service was at an end, the invalid and infirm, Lincoln's Camp Nelson even provided the Soldiers' Home, "to care for him who shall have borne the battle." Camp Nelson was only one of many of its kind, yet it contained in small compass all the elements of the organization, the system, the industry and enterprise, that made the war machine of the Union invincible in the end. (NA)

Fire and Stone

★ ★

Robert K. Krick

SINCE AN ARTILLERY PIECE fired the opening round of the Civil War in the direction of a fort, it is hardly surprising that so much of the war effort went into using artillery, on the one hand, and protecting against it with fortifications, on the other. That first shot in the early morning hours of April 12, 1861, was the signal for a concentrated bombardment of Fort Sumter in Charleston harbor. When the fort surrendered a day and a half later, it had been the target of about four thousand shot and shell. The delirious conquerors viewed the result as a stunning victory that validated the prowess of Southern arms. Few of the military men who witnessed the affair viewed it as a symptom of the changes afoot in both artillery and fortifications.

For decades before the war, the United States had been at work on a system of masonry fortifications that left the coastline speckled with forts of several standard patterns. Many army officers spent their antebellum careers building those forts; the rest spent their time manning them. R. E. Lee's service in the old army, for instance, included stints at work on construction of or improvements to Fort Pulaski near Savannah, Fort Carroll in Baltimore harbor, Fort Monroe in Virginia, and Fort Hamilton in New York harbor.

While fixed fortifications got their due in the 1850s, little attention was paid to the notion that field fortifications might become essential considerations in the next war. The Civil War was just about precisely half over before infantry began to entrench in earnest. By 1864, ad hoc protective works were thrown up routinely with or without guidance from engineer officers.

To some extent, field fortifications were designed for protection against artillery fire, and the fixed fortifications had such protection as their primary goal. The artillery delivering fire against Civil War targets was in the midst of a revolution in equipment, tactics, and ammunition. Artillery offered perhaps a greater variety of weapons specifically designed for specific purposes than any other category of weapons in the war.

Field artillery in the Mexican War and into the 1850s had consisted in large part of bronze 6-pounder and 12-pounder guns, and of lightweight bronze howitzers. The guns were too heavy to be adequately mobile, and the howitzers were short on range and power. A fresh design sponsored by Emperor Louis-Napoléon of France first was cast in America in 1857. The new 12-pounder bronze weapon weighed almost one-third less than the 12-pounder gun, and could do most of the things for which both guns and howitzers had been required in the past. Although there were fewer than a half-dozen of the "napoleon" on hand in 1861, it quickly became the favorite of Civil War artillerists on both sides. The napoleon could operate at as long a range as the heavy old 12-pounder gun, and was much more adept at firing shell and canister. Late in 1862, Lee was pleading with Richmond (at the instance of Stonewall Jackson) for napoleons, offering 6-pounders and old 12-pounders to be melted down for the metal if necessary. By the end of the war, there were about eighteen hundred napoleons in service.

An even more pivotal change in artillery also was in motion in the 1850s. The immense increase in range and accuracy that rifling granted to sporting weapons was something artillerists long had envied. Neither artillery nor military small arms, however, had been able to take advantage of rifling until just before the Civil War. The rifled sporting weapons had only marginal military application because they were cumbersome to load, requiring that a tight-fitting patch around the ball be hammered home to the base of the barrel. Only in that manner could the charge fit tightly enough to take the spin imparted by the spiral grooves of the rifling.

The advent of rifled muskets and of rifled artillery resulted in each case not from the design of new weapons, but rather from the design of new ammunition that could be loaded easily but still fit tightly on firing and thus pick up the rifling spin. It was just before 1860 when the first rifled artillery projectiles appeared in America. Some rounds were designed that required a precise fitting of studs on the sides of the projectile into the grooves of the rifle. Inevitably this system resulted in very careful — and therefore very slow — loading; it also required exquisitely careful manufacture and handwork.

The rifled artillery projectiles that revolutionized artillery practice were those that expanded into the rifled grooves only at the moment of firing, and therefore went into the gun loosely and yet fit tightly on the way out. The expansion at firing did not involve the entire projectile, of course. A band or cup of soft metal such as lead or brass or copper was affixed to the round in such a way that the gases from the propellant charge pushed the soft metal out into the rifling. Imaginative designs proliferated amongst ordnance dabblers on both sides. The Confederates actually tried a projectile with wings attached, so that it would spin in flight even after being fired from a smoothbore.

Charles T. James was one of the men at work on rifled artillery. He contrived a method for converting bronze smoothbore guns to rifles by boring narrow, deep grooves into them. Guns so fixed became known as James rifles. Because bronze is a soft metal, the rifling in the James pieces didn't stand up well, and iron quickly became the metal of choice in rifles. Robert P. Parrott patented in 1861 a design for a rifle made of cast iron, with a wrought-iron band shrunk around the breech for reinforcement at the point of greatest pressure. The resulting 10-pounder and 20-pounder Parrotts were mainstays of artillerists on the battlefields of the Civil War. Their familiar forms dot those fields to this day, readily distinguishable by the reinforcement ring around the breech.

The 10-pounder Parrott was overshadowed in large measure as the war progressed by an even better piece. The 3-inch ordnance rifle was made of tough wrought iron and performed admirably in the field. A young Virginia artillerist, Ned Moore, came up against this "most accurate shooter" for the first time at Cedar Mountain in August 1862, and remarked upon the "singular noise" made by its shells: "quite like the shrill note of a tree-frog on a big scale." Those shrill shells went where they were aimed with a precision that gratified their employers. The longer range and greater accuracy of rifled pieces were obvious advantages. For close work, though, the napoleon fired more metal from a larger bore; and when canister was the specific, rifles were not as useful. As a result, a well-run artillery battalion included some rifles and some napoleons.

The men who led this new field artillery on both sides of the lines included a host of youngsters whose bravery made them legendary. Capt. Hubert Dilger, who went by the catchy nickname Leatherbreeches, made an immortal name for himself at Chancellorsville as he stood undaunted against Stonewall Jackson's mighty flank attack. Dilger was reported to have fallen back down the Orange Turnpike only by means of the recoil of his pieces, on a day when most of his comrades were fleeing incontinently. At Gettysburg, Charles E. Hazlett was mortally wounded while working his guns on Little Round Top with all eyes upon him, and Alonzo H. Cushing died in epic dramatic circumstances at the focus of Maj. Gen. George E. Pickett's charge.

Willie Pegram constantly fought his Confederate guns from positions beyond friendly infantry lines. His bespectacled face was shining "with the fire of battle" on Hazel Grove at Chancellorsville as he called across the guns to a comrade: "A glorious day, Colonel, a glorious day." None of the war's artillerists glowed with a special fire any more brightly than did John Pelham of Alabama — "the gallant" Pelham, Lee called him after Fredericksburg. Pelham was only a major when he died before the war was half over, and he was only twenty-four years old, but something about him appeals strongly across the years. A sizable and zealous Pelham society thrives a century and a quarter later.

Men of higher rank in artillery service had a profound effect on the war. Gen. Henry J. Hunt, for instance, was arguably one of the most important men in the Army of the Potomac, which he served as artillery chief for much of the war. His admirable skills in organization and operations made that army's long arm wonderfully efficient. By exiling Hunt to rear areas during the Chancellorsville campaign, Joe Hooker went far toward losing that battle. The opposing Army of Northern Virginia, by contrast, had Gen. William Nelson Pendleton, a querulous, stodgy, and ineffective fellow, as nominal head of its artillery.

Not all of the dire disadvantages that beset Southern artillerists are well recognized. Shortages of material and of industrial capacity in the South do get well-deserved attention. Desperate efforts to increase such output found mixed success at best. Catherine Furnace, which became a landmark on the Chancellorsville battlefield, illustrates the problem well. The furnace had failed economically in the 1840s after a decade of weak output — the victim of poor-grade bog ore. The Confederacy started Catherine Furnace anew but it never made even so simple a product as artillery solid shot, yielding only pig iron to send to Richmond's overworked manufactories.

Less familiar is the tale of woeful results achieved by Confederate artillery ammunition. Despite the best efforts of the country's ordnance wizard, Josiah Gorgas, Confederate explosive shells just did not go off with any reliability. Imaginative ersatz devices intended to ensure ignition often failed. A Confederate artillerist who fought through the finest artillery performance of the Army of Northern Virginia at Chancellorsville reported in the aftermath:

I found our fuses were very defective, although it was reported to me that we were using the fuse-igniter. I estimated that one of our shell out of fifteen exploded. . . . I was compelled to watch closely the effect of all the projectiles, as if we were using entirely solid shot.

Confederate rifled rounds were particularly defective, tumbling in flight and failing to explode or else exploding prematurely. E. P. Alexander, who was among the very finest of Confederate artillerymen, refused to use any rifled guns except in one single battery of the six in his battalion. In evaluating the problem of premature explosions, Alexander explained that the army's tactics were damaged by the basic inability to fire over advancing friendly troops. Southern infantry knew "by sad experience" of the danger in such a practice, and Alexander claimed that he had "known of their threatening to fire back at our guns if we opened over their heads." Solid shot could be used safely for the purpose, but that was the least effective sort of round. Furthermore, the infantry wouldn't know the difference and "would be demoralized & angry all the same."

One artillery advantage that the South realized was organizational. Since time immemorial, batteries had been assigned to brigades until the two became almost an integral unit. This left an infantry officer with considerable power over the artillery captain. Efficient use of the artillery too often gave way to considerations of unit pride, and to the vagaries affecting brigade locations. During the winter of 1862/63, the Army of Northern Virginia scrapped this inept system and instituted a battalion organization based on groupings of four to six batteries. Two field officers and a staff hierarchy went with each battalion. E. P. Alexander, who had been a central figure in crafting the new arrangement, was so delighted with his battalion that he at first refused to be considered for an opportunity as brigadier general of infantry, saying that his battalion was as "independent & as conspicuous as a Division of Infantry." Most of Alexander's comrades doubtless would have cheerfully subscribed to his notion that six hundred artillerymen and their guns were more than the equivalent of eight thousand infantrymen. The Union artillery copied the battalion idea before long, and eventually most of the armies of Europe did too.

By 1865, there were field fortifications everywhere a handful of soldiers had gathered. Early in the war, however, no one thought to throw some earth or some wood between themselves and the long-range rifled arms that were aimed their way. Many of the men, in fact, were derisive of such cowardly measures. When R. E. Lee assumed command of the army he would make famous, one of his first initiatives was to fortify the Confederate lines around Richmond as a means to free manpower for offensive action. The response of his army was strongly negative. Lee was "The King of Spades," it was said, and must be short on the daring and aggressiveness that the South needed.

An observant veteran soldier from South Carolina reported that until December 13, 1862, his unit had never built any protective works. That night, after the Battle of Fredericksburg was actually over, "the brigade felled a few trees and formed a rude breastwork — the first thing of the kind we ever lay behind." When campaigning opened again the next spring, the same young man found himself behind the same "rude breastwork." This time he noticed among his comrades "the first well-defined inclination for protection in battle." On that day, the war was already three weeks more than half over.

Visitors to the scenes of Civil War action often use the earthworks as benchmarks to discern what happened. As surviving traces of what soldiers themselves did long ago, the earthworks also are touchstones — points of departure for our imaginations. Photographs of the works as they stood in the 1860s show complex, sometimes massive defenses. The same works today often are far less sizable. The reason in most cases is that the men using them for protection employed logs and other wood for the main mass of their work. That wood fiber is long gone today, but the earthen mounds remain as mute reminders of the men who fought behind and around them.

Field fortifications also have changed from their original appearance because they suffered rapid alterations every time they changed hands. There was, of course, a front and a back side to each fortification. If one army abandoned a line, or was driven from it, the new owners hurried to fill in one side of the work and scoop out the other. Modern visitors to old battlefields who become confused can take solace in the account of a young Virginian from Orange County. George Q. Peyton had fought near the "Bloody Angle" at Spotsylvania behind earthworks that were among the most complex (and perhaps the most famous) field fortifications built during the war. A week after the famous day at the Bloody Angle, Pvt. Peyton wrote in his diary that his regiment "occupied our old line of works near where we fought. . . . The Yanks had filled up the ditches and turned the works around so I hardly knew them."

Formal fixed fortifications were proving less and less imposing at the same time that field fortifications were growing in use and importance. During February 1862, Confederates suffered the loss of control of both the Cumberland and Tennessee rivers when Forts Henry and Donelson could not stand up to Gen. U. S. Grant. Not long thereafter, at the same Fort Pulaski in Georgia that R. E. Lee had helped to build as a youthful lieutenant, Northern weapons signaled a new day in warfare. On April 10 and 11, 1862, some of the gigantic new siege rifles, under Gen. Q. A. Gillmore, shattered the brick walls of the fort with amazing ease and in rather short time. It was apparent that big rifles could batter down masonry walls from a far greater distance than the designers of those walls had imagined possible.

Two masonry fortifications protecting the approaches to

New Orleans also fell in April 1862 — Fort Jackson and Fort Saint Philip. When they succumbed to Federal firepower and seapower, the South's largest city followed suit promptly. Forts Gaines and Morgan and Powell were similarly impotent in protecting Mobile in 1864. The arsenals of the North were stocking weapons unlike anything used in earlier wars: 200-pounder Parrotts; 300-pounder Parrotts; 13-inch mortars; 8-inch, 10-inch, and 15-inch Rodman smoothbores; even 20-inch Rodmans, the biggest guns ever cast in the country, albeit guns that never were used. It was apparent that fortifications would have to change in keeping with the changes in what was being thrown at them.

Forts built of earth proved to be an interesting and often successful expedient. Their earthen walls absorbed the same mammoth bolts that crumbled masonry walls. Fort Sumter itself illustrated the case to some extent when it was the focus of a mighty Federal attack in 1863. Its masonry walls quickly were reduced to a pile of rubble bearing little resemblance to the fort of 1861. The rubble pile became virtually a pile of dirt, however, and was almost impervious to further harm. Confederate Battery Wagner, across the harbor from Sumter, was built mostly of Carolina sand and fell only after desperate, close infantry action.

The Confederates held a critical strong point on the James River below Richmond at Drewry's Bluff through the war. The fort atop that bluff had earthen walls, and also was blessed with a panoramic view down the river. Confederate artillery atop the bluff drove back Union gunboats on the river in May 1862 at a time when there was uncertainty whether Richmond could be held. Two years later another battle at Drewry's Bluff resulted in another Confederate victory, this time predominantly as a result of infantry action.

A splendid example of the new earthen fortification at work came at Knoxville, Tennessee, during James Longstreet's bungled attack on the Federals there in November of 1863. A small earthwork near the city was named Fort Sanders, in honor of a Northern officer killed earlier that month. After much equivocation, Longstreet determined to launch an infantry assault on the fort after artillery preparation. Confederate rifled artillery firing at Fort Sanders (with the usual ineffective ammunition) failed to make any impression. The tiny group of Northerners in the fort then beat back a large contingent of proud infantry veterans of the Army of Northern Virginia with consummate ease on November 29. The Southerners engaged lost not only a painfully large number of soldiers but also considerable poise, because the reverse set off an attack of biliousness in Longstreet that resulted in charges against his ranking subordinate. Fort Sanders did the Confederacy much harm.

As Confederate access to the world shriveled late in the war, the last gateway for blockade-runners was Wilmington, North Carolina. A fortification of earth and sand named Fort Fisher held that portal open. Thunderous, rolling bombardments failed to shake the place; only maneuverable infantry would be able to isolate and neutralize the fort. A vast Federal expedition mounted in December 1864 failed to take Fort Fisher, but a renewed effort the next month captured the stronghold on January 15, 1865.

By the time of the Fort Fisher expeditions, the war in Virginia had long since settled into virtual siege operations around Petersburg. What had started as field fortifications when units went to ground in the summer of 1864 had turned into endless miles of mighty works, defended by abatis and chevaux-de-frise and traverses and all the other implements of the entrenchers' art. Infantry lines were dotted with artillery redoubts and with strong earthen forts. These forts often were named for the commander in the area, or for a recently dead hero. The soldiers sometimes gave the forts vivid names, such as the aptly labeled Fort Hell near Petersburg. Lee's last offensive gesture during the war in Virginia came against one such work, Fort Stedman. A stealthy attack on the morning of March 25 won temporary success but degenerated into demoralizing defeat. Within a week, Lee was away from the miles of forts and fortifications around Petersburg and racing in vain for Lynchburg until he was brought up short at Appomattox Court House.

Four years of war had worked nothing less than a revolution

in fortification and artillery. Napoleons and 3-inch ordnance rifles and 20-pounder Parrott rifles had supplanted a series of far less efficient pieces. Mammoth siege weapons had demonstrated the impotence of masonry forts. Artillery battalions had destroyed the parochial notion that batteries and brigades made a team. Soldiers under fire had resolved the need for protection by refining a system of field fortifications. And the North had won its war, not least because of its skillful exploitation of the mechanical and industrial capacity that made its artillery a force on land and sea.

In a scene repeated innumerable times on both sides in the war, members of a battery division from the Army of the Potomac, in this case one with some sixteen or more cannons, draw themselves into line for the photographer outside their winter quarters. While no accurate tally exists, it is probable that men like these manned more than five thousand artillery pieces of varying kinds in this war. (USAMHI)

Headquarters of the mighty Union artillery effort was the Washington Arsenal, where every day a seemingly endless array of weapons awaited shipment to Lincoln's far-flung armies. (LC)

Across the lines, their Confederate foes had to depend largely upon what they could buy, take from the Yankees, sneak through the blockade, or manufacture. As a result, much of Rebel gunnery involved more outdated pieces, like this captured 12-pounder field howitzer shown in 1862. (USAMHI)

The Union, too, had its share of outmoded weapons, like these 12-pounder mountain howitzers shown in Fayetteville, Arkansas, probably in the hands of men of the Third Kansas Light Artillery. (WCHS)

Men everywhere went to fight with what they had, like these youngsters still awaiting their uniforms, but with an old field piece to take off to war. (JAH)

The workhorse cannon of the war would be the napoleon field piece, like these two in the foreground being served by men of Company F of the Third Massachusetts Heavy Artillery. Photographer W. M. Smith made this image at Fort Stevens, in the defenses of Washington, in August 1865, with the war done, and when the men had time to polish their cannons brightly. (LC)

Confederates often cast their own napoleons, like these pieces captured from them on Missionary Ridge in November 1863, and here photographed in Chattanooga. (NA)

More accurate and with greater range, the 3-inch ordnance rifle was also popular in both armies. This piece was used by the Rebels until captured with Petersburg in April 1865. Its captors pose jauntily upon the now forever-silent cannon. (LC)

Still more deadly, and manufactured in a seemingly endless variety of sizes, was the Parrott rifle, marked by its distinctive reinforcing band around the breech. This 3.67-inch Parrott field piece was a favorite throughout the Union army. (LC)

More intimidating was the 30-pounder, like this brace of Parrotts in Fort Putnam, among the Federal works surrounding Charleston. Their power, especially against masonry fortifications, was awesome. Yankee cameramen Haas & Peale made the Parrotts around Charleston the most photographed of the war. (USAMHI)

Top left: Fort Putnam had even larger guns, like these massive 100-pounder Parrotts, shown in 1865 with their shells. (LC)

Top right: And nearby in Battery Hays, one of the batteries that severely reduced Fort Sumter, Haas & Peale found this huge 200-pounder. Even larger types were cast. (NYHS)

Among the larger guns, the variety seemed endless, particularly in the case of those intended for seacoast defense. Here a 32-pounder seacoast gun does duty in one of Washington's many forts. (USAMHI)

Two more large siege guns stand in Richmond after the city's fall in 1865. At left is a 32-pounder Navy smoothbore, and next to it, a 6.4-inch rifle. Behind them a host of other captured Confederate field pieces and siege guns await shipment north. (LC)

The Confederates made some of their own distinctive big guns, like this 7-inch, double-banded Brooke rifle in Mobile's Fort Morgan. The bands reinforcing the breech allowed for heavier powder charges. (NA)

In Battery Marion at Charleston's Fort Moultrie, a triple-banded 7-inch Brooke helped to protect the Confederacy's vital South Carolina harbor. (USAMHI)

Some of the South's larger weapons were purchased abroad, like this 150-pounder Armstrong gun in Fort Fisher, near Wilmington, North Carolina. (USAMHI)

Less gripping on the public imagination were the ponderous mortars used for battering fortresses and cities. Batteries like these helped reduce Confederate works around Charleston. (USAMHI)

A massive Yankee water battery at Gloucester Point, Virginia, near Yorktown, mounted fifteen mortars that pounded Confederate positions in 1862. Eight of them show here. Their gunners could not even see their targets, having to depend upon word from "spotters" to learn if their aim was true. (USAMHI)

No single cannon of the war became better known than this 13-inch mortar mounted on a flatbed rail car. Called "Dictator," it was only one of many of its size, but this one happened to interest a photographer, who repeatedly captured its image — as here, near Petersburg, Virginia, on September 1, 1864. The photographer, Timothy O'Sullivan, made the gun famous. (USAMHI)

Top left: Ingenuity did not end with the big guns. Scores of new designs were tried. A few worked; most did not. One that failed was the Confederate double-barreled cannon made in Georgia. (CWTIC)

Top right: Another failure was this volley gun, designed to send dozens of bullets at an enemy in a single firing. (NA)

One that did work, though its use was limited to one battery, was the Requia volley gun, whose multiple barrels could send forth a wall of lead several feet wide. (NA)

Sometimes ingenuity combined size with mobility, as with this banded siege gun
mounted on a fortified flatcar. It could be moved quickly anywhere there were rails.
(USAMHI)

The really huge guns were reserved for defending seacoast forts from ship-borne attack. A massive 9-inch Dahlgren gun peers out to sea. (USAMHI)

An even larger 15-inch Dahlgren sits ready in the Washington defenses in August 1864. A small man could fit into its bore. (USAMHI)

Biggest of all the guns were the massive
Rodman columbiads. A modest 10-inch
Confederate Rodman copy sits in its
emplacement near the James River. (USAMHI)

Another, Yankee, Rodman stares silently
from the parapet of New York City's
Fort Columbus in 1865. The largest gun of
the war was a 20-inch Rodman that was
never fired in anger. (NA)

While the artillery of the Civil War represented much that was new, it also put an end to much of the old in the science of fortifications. The old Union had rimmed its seacoasts with masonry fortifications like Fort Monroe, off Virginia's Hampton Roads. (NA)

Conceived and built in a time when there was less powerful artillery to contend with, these massive brick or stone edifices, like Fort Jefferson in the Dry Tortugas off Florida, were already obsolete in 1861. (USAMHI)

Some of the fortresses, like Fort Sumter —
and Fort Jefferson, shown here — were still
under construction when the war began. (LC)

Yet North and South alike rushed to
maintain or seize possession of them when
the call to arms came. Neither expected the
effect that newly developed heavy-caliber
guns and exploding shells would have. Fort
Sumter, photographed by Charleston
cameramen Osborn & Durbec on April 17,
1861, three days after its fall, shows on its
land side only a little of the damage done. (LC)

Fire from Rebel batteries on Morris Island severely battered the southwest angle of the fort. (TU)

This faded, previously unpublished Osborn & Durbec image shows the terreplein on the western face of the fort, well mauled by the Charleston batteries. (TU)

The fort's commander, Maj. Robert Anderson, had no choice but to surrender his beleaguered garrison. Shown here sometime later, standing fifth from the left, as a brigadier general, he poses inside a Northern seacoast fort that has obviously never felt the sting of Confederate cannons. (JAH)

Fort Pulaski, protecting Savannah, was another seemingly impregnable bastion. Its thick walls and ominous columbiads, shown here in 1863, presented a formidable face to any attacker. The Confederates seized the fort in January 1861 when an ill-prepared Washington had left it in the hands of a single sergeant! (USAMHI)

Fifteen months later, on April 10 and 11, 1862, when the Federals came back to reclaim it, Yankee siege guns took just two days to pound these two massive holes through its walls, making it untenable. The fort surrendered, and the days of masonry fortifications were clearly over. (NA)

If further proof were needed, it came at Fort Morgan, on Mobile Bay. Built to prevent an enemy from entering the harbor, it could do nothing as a Union fleet steamed right past it on August 5, 1864. (NA)

That allowed the Federals to land troops to invest the fort, and after a brief siege, it, too, fell to their hands. (NA)

But no forts in the South came even close to the massive damage received by those at Charleston, South Carolina. Fort Moultrie on Sullivans Island was blasted repeatedly. (USAMHI)

And Fort Sumter was left a shapeless pile of rubble by late 1864. (TU)

Confederate photographer George S. Cook took his camera inside the besieged fortress in 1864 to record its chaotic interior, with gun carriages blown from the now demolished terreplein, holes in the walls, and devastation everywhere. (USAMHI)

After its final fall in 1865, Sumter bore no resemblance at all to the imposing fortress of 1861. (USAMHI)

This image, made about April 14, 1865, the fourth anniversary of the fort's fall to the Confederates, shows more eloquently than words how little was left of the bastion Anderson tried so nobly to defend. (LC)

Top left: Other, less formal, more adaptable defenses against enemy artillery and bullets evolved quickly as the war progressed, and often they were more effective than walls of stone and mortar. Ironically, Confederates even used cotton at times. In 1862, erecting defenses at Yorktown, Rebels incorporated cotton bales into their fortifications. (USAMHI)

Top right: The previous fall, out at Lexington, Missouri, Confederates led by Gen. Sterling Price created probably the war's only mobile fortress when they erected a wall of hemp bales and slowly pushed it ahead of them as they advanced and finally took the town. A previously unpublished portrait of Price taken sometime after March 1862. (ADAH)

Bottom right: Very quickly the Rebels learned to protect their rivers with earthworks like these at Yorktown, and quickly, too, they learned that dirt and sandbags were far more effective against shot and shell than were brick and stone. (USAMHI)

The Rebels soon had the York River almost lined with earth-protected batteries like this one mounting several Parrott rifles. (USAMHI)

Battery 4 off Yorktown was another example. This one even sprouted grass, which had the added benefit of somewhat camouflaging its emplacements. (USAMHI)

Both sides built even larger earth-and-sand forts farther to the south. Fort Putnam on Morris Island was originally built as Battery Gregg by the Confederates, then was captured and strengthened by the Yankees. Haas & Peale photographed it in 1863. (USAMHI)

Walls of earth could be built thicker, stronger, and quicker by far than anything previously seen in American warfare. (USAMHI)

Shells that, upon exploding, might send hundreds of dangerous fragments of brick flying about in a regular fort like Sumter, here just harmlessly buried themselves in the sand or kicked up clouds of annoying but hardly dangerous debris. (AIG)

Of course, such new kinds of forts called for
very different amenities for their defenders.
Soldiers' quarters were not the safe and
comfortable casemates or barracks of a
Pulaski, but simply tents. (USAMHI)

It was no different for the officers. (USAMHI)

The interior was strictly utilitarian, and the men lived close to their guns. (USAMHI)

Such earthwork forts could even appear in cities. At Vanderhoff's Wharf in Charleston, this earthen battery appeared right on the edge of the city, along the Cooper River. (NYHS)

The least permanent fortifications in this war were those thrown up hastily on the battlefield, and at first neither side used them. Indeed, perhaps the first fieldworks of the war were these built by Confederates to protect Centreville, Virginia, during the winter of 1861/62. They were armed in places with "quaker guns"—nothing more than logs, which from a distance looked like cannons pointing out from the embrasures. (USAMHI)

The first major battle use of field fortifications came at Fredericksburg in December 1862. Sitting behind earthen works like these, Rebels peered across the Rappahannock as the Federals crossed the river and fruitlessly attacked the well-protected defenders. (NA)

Out west Confederates used such works to even better advantage as they protected the bluffs along the Mississippi. Their earthworks lined the high banks at Port Hudson, Louisiana, the last major bastion on the river to fall to the Yankees. (NA)

While there was always a sense of disorder about these less formal fortresses, there was no contesting their power to resist an enemy. Even Port Hudson fell only when surrounded and starved into submission. Its walls were never breached. (NA)

Perhaps the most extensive, and one of the most formidable, of the Confederate earthworks was Fort Fisher, off Wilmington, North Carolina. Shown here in an 1865 image by Timothy O'Sullivan, it never succumbed to bombardment but, like most others of its kind, collapsed when its garrison was out of guns and outnumbered three-to-one. (CHS)

By 1864 men of both sides were expert in erecting defenses for their most immediate needs of protection. In only a few hours, logs and earth could be turned into works like these Northern fortifications now being used by two Federal batteries outside Petersburg. (USAMHI)

When more time was available, the earth could be bagged and packed more carefully. A June 20, 1864, image of the First New York Artillery in just-captured Rebel works at Petersburg. (USAMHI)

The more time allowed, the more extensive the works could become. Haas & Peale's 1863 image shows the first parallel in what would be a series of earthworks the Federals used to push their lines gradually forward on Morris Island. Using one line as a base, engineers could send trenches running forward, then connect them laterally to create a new line a few yards closer to the enemy. (USAMHI)

And given several months in a siege, men could do what the Confederates did here around Petersburg — create a virtual maze of forts and earthworks. (LC)

The Federals besieging them had just as much time, and their works — neater, to be sure — stretched as far as the eye could see. (USAMHI)

Looking toward the horizon from the captured Rebel works after April 1865, one could see line after line of successive works — testimony to the ingenuity of the engineers, and the endless toil of the soldiers. (USAMHI)

Bombproofs and subterranean passages often connected one fort with another, while powder magazines like this one were buried beneath ten feet or more of sandbags and "gabions," wicker baskets filled with earth. (USAMHI)

Gabions and chevaux-de-frise — lines of sharpened stakes — protected the Confederate Fort Mahone, which its opponents soon dubbed Fort Damnation. It appears here on April 3, 1865, the day after the Petersburg works fell. (USAMHI)

The Yankee forts at Petersburg looked much the same, as here at Fort Rice. The shelter tents that had provided roofs for the winter huts have already been removed from the ridge poles of the soldiers' quarters, showing just how impermanent these works were meant to be. This image was also made very shortly after Petersburg fell, and already the Yankees have abandoned their works. (USAMHI)

The Confederates were beaten and on the run everywhere, and even their dauntless fortifications — crude yet effective new weapons for defense in a landscape of war now forever changed — could not stand indefinitely. Everywhere they fell. Often the Rebels themselves destroyed their magazines and dismounted their guns as they fled. (LC)

Sometimes their guns lay where they had exploded after heavy use. (USAMHI)

Sometimes no one would remember whether it was friend or foe who destroyed their now silent cannons. (USAMHI)

With the fall of the Confederacy, its artillery was gathered, as here at Richmond, and sent north, prizes to the victors. (USAMHI)

Like this half-buried columbiad in George N. Barnard's image of Sumter in 1866, they and the forts they had protected were about to disappear from a scene where once they had been terrible. (CWTIC)

Their man-made thunder, which had echoed around the world and down through the decades, was never to be heard again. (USAMHI)

Billy Yank

A portfolio of the Union
fighting man in camp and field

Top left: Before 1861, there had been busby-wearing militiamen like the Lowell Light Infantry. (JAH)

Top right: National Lancers who looked like something from the time of Napoleon. (JAH)

Militiamen with feathers and epaulets. (JAH)

But in 1861 the call was answered by tens of thousands who knew nothing of such soldiering. They were farm boys, mechanics, clerks, sons of noble fathers and the offspring of fathers undistinguished, all bound by a common cause: youth, adventure, and the Union. Recruits gather at the corner of High and Walnut streets in Morgantown, Virginia, soon to be West Virginia. (WVU)

Regiments were raised quickly, and well before many were ready they were sent off to the war, among them the Sixty-ninth New York. It took its first and only blooding in its three months' service at Bull Run. Here, six days later, it returns to New York and a parade down Broadway — with forty-five of its men left dead on the fields of Virginia. It was a rude first lesson in warfare. (FL)

Out with the western armies, the boys were little different. Whether here in the barracks of the 124th Illinois at Vicksburg . . . (USAMHI)

. . . or here, photographed by French & Company in the barracks of the Fifty-second U.S. Colored Infantry at Vicksburg, Billy Yank was Billy Yank. (KA)

He was looser in his dress than his eastern brethren. Like the Forty-seventh Illinois here in Mississippi, he preferred a slouch hat to the more military short-billed kepi worn in the Army of the Potomac. (WMA)

His specialty, as with soldiers of all armies, at all times, was relaxation. When ninety percent of a soldier's time was spent finding ways to fill free hours, he could become expert. (USAMHI)

Wherever he went, there was always time to sit, light a pipe, read a letter, pose for the camera, build a winter hut, or fashion a rude bench. (USAMHI)

In the shadow of war's destruction, he pitched his tent. (USAMHI)

Relaxation, in all its forms, occupied more of Billy Yank's time in a single month than all the time spent in battle during the entire war. Boredom sometimes became a greater enemy than the Rebels. (TF)

Many found solace in liquor, and every camp had its sutlers anxious to ply their wares from their tents and makeshift bars. (JAH)

Top left: But mostly they simply talked, refought their old battles . . . (JAH)

Top right: . . . frolicked when they could . . . (JAH)

. . . or talked of the battles to come. George D. Wells of the Thirty-fourth Massachusetts could muse with the newspapermen on either side of him about the fighting ahead. One of those battles, at Cedar Creek in the Shenandoah Valley, would end his boredom forever. (USAMHI)

A few of them were older fellows, like old Pvt. Truman Head of the First United States Sharpshooters, who was better known as California Joe. A noted marksman from the West, he is said to have made a will at the war's start, leaving $50,000 for the care of disabled Billy Yanks in case of his death in the war. "Entirely free from brag and bluster," wrote a comrade, Head "was one of those splendid characters that made him a hero in spite of himself." The same might have been said of Billy Yank in all his guises. (VHS)

But mostly they were young, like their puppy mascot, and sprouting their first beards. (USAMHI)

They performed all kinds of duties. Some, like Mike Crowley of the Twelfth Massachusetts, were teamsters, caring for the mules . . . (USAMHI)

. . . and driving the wagons and carts that carried water and the soldiers' impedimenta. (USAMHI)

No one was more resplendent than a military
drum major. (JAH)

He could look and dress like what the
innocent prewar boys thought a soldier ought
to appear. (JAH)

Top left: The twitter of the fife was never forgotten, nor the sight of the fifer in his musician's frock coat. (JAH)

Top right: Neither was the sound of the rotary valve horn, . . . (JAH)

. . . especially if it was a booming giant like this one. Music meant a lot to Billy Yank. (JAH)

Top left: Burnside's Rhode Island Zouaves were among the earliest in the service, and one of the most colorful. (JAH)

Top right: The headgear could be marvelous, if hardly utilitarian. (JAH)

A near relation to the zouave was the chasseur, such as this one from the Eighty-third Pennsylvania. Ostensibly trained for very rapid movement, the chasseur in this war was an infantryman like everyone else. (JAH)

Top left: Another chasseur — this one holding a Volcanic pistol, an early progenitor of the Henry and Winchester rifles. (JAH)

Top right: But most Billy Yanks looked like this corporal ready for the field, all his equipment in place, rifle at his side. (JAH)

The lads liked to sit for the camera and display their weapons. Half of soldiering, some thought, was striking the right martial attitude. This boy holds a sharpshooter's rifle with telescopic sight mounted on its side. Such weapons were rare, and were used almost exclusively in special units. (JAH)

Top left: Most Yanks, like this "Bucktail" from a Pennsylvania regiment, used a standard Springfield or Enfield rifle. (JAH)

Top right: Quite possibly this fellow is a sharpshooter himself, since he holds a Sharps rifle with special double-set triggers used by marksmen. (JAH)

The cavalrymen were no different from their counterparts on foot. When they could, they sat astride their mounts for the camera, like this trooper with his .44-caliber Colt model 1860 revolver pointed, it is to be hoped, toward the foe. (JAH)

Yet the mounted men could sit for the camera atop things far more lofty than their horses. Men of this unidentified Yankee outfit perch on Point Lookout on Tennessee's Lookout Mountain, clutching their Spencer carbines and their sabers, hats, and flag. (RFC)

Top left: Now and then a Billy Yank looked like a host in himself, with his Colt, his saber, and even a rare Hall saddle carbine in his lap. That was a lot of hardware to take to war. (JAH)

Top right: They posed with their comrades and tentmates, like these two Rhode Islanders in Burnside blouses and holding Burnside carbines. (JAH)

The zouaves did it. (JAH)

Cavalrymen did it—the one at right leaning on an early model Henry repeating rifle. (JAH)

Bandsmen did it, horns at their sides as if they were weapons at the ready. (JAH)

They sat for the camera. (JAH)

Even ate for the camera, crunching on their
hardtack — so-called army bread. (JAH)

They posed in threes, like these New York Fire Zouaves. (JAH)

And showed off their ceremonial parade swords. (JAH)

Crossing barriers of rank, officers and
enlisted men posed together and, if this image
may be believed, shared a bottle and cigars
now and then. (JAH)

They followed their beloved flags and made
their colors renowned — none more so than
those of the Iron Brigade, its battle credits
for the battles of Gainesville, Second
Bull Run, South Mountain, Antietam,
Fredericksburg, and Gettysburg proudly
displayed. (JAH)

Often their banners showed not only where the flags had been, but that the journey had not been an easy one. The colors of the Eighth Pennsylvania Reserves. (USAMHI)

It was not an easy journey for Billy Yank, either, but he faced it squarely, resolutely. (USAMHI)

Bottom left: He risked death from the plains of Manassas to the heights of Lookout Mountain. (JAH)

Bottom right: He did it for fun, for adventure, for love of country and of those left at home, whose photographs he carried with him — or simply because he was drafted and had no choice. (JAH)

Whatever his reasons, he did the job he was given. (JAH)

He went to war a beardless boy, full of innocence and wonder. (JAH)

And came home bloodied, scarred—like the colors of the Thirty-third New Jersey—no longer innocent, but ennobled. (TO)

Everyone's War

★ ★

Emory M. Thomas

THE WAR commenced for Billy Yank as a simple conflict about union. Abraham Lincoln called out 75,000 militia troops to confront "combinations too powerful to be suppressed by the ordinary course of judicial proceedings, or by the powers vested in the [U.S.] marshals by law." Jefferson Davis responded by calling for 100,000 men and asserting, "All we want is to be let alone." The American Civil War did not continue so relatively uncomplicated. In four bloody years the war touched countless lives, and the scope of war itself approached totality.

Directly involved in the war were many more people than those 175,000 citizen-soldiers mobilized by Lincoln and Davis in April 1861. And of those involved there were many who were not native-born white American men. Drawn into the conflict were Indians, Mexican-Americans, European immigrants, Afro-Americans, and women. Understanding the enormous impact of the war requires an appreciation of the involvement of these "minorities" and an understanding of the degrees to which the experience of wartime transformed their lives and place in American society.

That society had long made an outcast of the Indian, yet almost from the beginning, the war between rival societies of white Americans also divided red Americans. The principal concentration of Indians close to the conflict inhabited the Indian Territory (the present state of Oklahoma). Known as the Five Civilized Tribes, some of these Indians were slaveholders and so felt some sympathy for the Confederacy, and many associated the Union with the policies by which they had lost their land and with the unkept promises that littered their relations with whites.

Of course Southern whites had also contributed to the Indians' plight, but in 1861 Confederates actively pursued an alliance with the Five Civilized Tribes and seemed to offer some change in what the Indians considered an oppressive status quo. Brig. Gen. Albert Pike, the Confederate commissioned for the task, concluded several treaties with various groups of Indians during the summer of 1861. The Confederacy pledged that Indians would not "hence forward . . . be in any wise troubled or molested by any power or people, State or person whatever."

Cherokee leader Stand Watie proved to be one of the most enthusiastic Confederate Indians. Watie also had signed the treaty that launched the "trail of tears" from Georgia to the Territory, however, and so his support for the Confederacy made him suspect among his people. John Ross, another Cherokee, led an Indian faction committed to remain loyal to the United States. Ross's followers, roughly half the inhabitants of the Indian Territory, tended to be full-blooded Indians; Watie's Confederates were most often of mixed blood.

As long as the United States Army remained preoccupied with missions outside the Territory, Pike and the Confederacy exerted considerable influence among the Indians. Stand Watie recruited three regiments of Indians for the Southern army and Pike led them into action in the Battle of Pea Ridge on March 7, 1862. The Indians, however, saw no good reason to remain on open ground while Federal artillery fired at them; so they took to the woods, where they might fight in a fashion more becoming common sense. After this experience Stand Watie's regiments returned to the Territory and fought an Indian version of the Civil War against pro-Union Indians there.

When the Federals finally sent cavalry units into the Indian Territory, the Confederates proved unable to uphold their pledge to keep their Indian allies from being "troubled or molested." Pike's urgent appeals to Richmond went unanswered, and in November 1862 he resigned. Fighting continued sporadically, though, between the supporters of Watie and Ross. For his efforts Watie became a Confederate brigadier general, and in June 1865 he became the last Southern general to surrender.

The Indians never exerted a truly significant impact upon the war, and neither did the other largely native-American group who served. In a strictly literal sense, all people born in Texas before the revolution in 1836 were Mexican-Americans. And the same logic applied more readily to residents of what became the Mexican Cession in 1848 following the Mexican War. Most Texans, however, had considered themselves "temporary" Mexicans at best, and in Confederate Texas friction continued between Anglos and genuine Mexican-Americans. Elsewhere, in New Mexico, Arizona, and California, Mexican-Americans divided between North and South. Landowners who practiced peonage tended to identify with the Confederacy. New Mexican Miguel Antonio Otero, Sr., plotted briefly to form a separate Pacific confederacy while North and South warred in the East. Both Confederate and Union armies had Mexican-American volunteers and conscripted troops.

Prominent among Mexican-American participants in the Civil War was Salvador Vallejo, who led a Union cavalry battalion of Californians that patrolled the Mexican border and fought Apaches. On the Confederate side Juan Quintero became a valuable diplomat. He secured friendly trade relations with Governor Santiago Vidaurri of Nuevo León and oversaw the passage of war supplies into Texas from Matamoros and northern Mexico in exchange for Confederate cotton.

Far more numerous than Mexican-American and Indian participants in the war were European-born immigrants to North America. Although the roots of the sectional quarrel lay deep within the early life of the American republic and the very name American Civil War implied a struggle between native-born rivals, the country had ever been a nation of immigrants. Thus it should not be surprising that immigrants played a significant part in the conflict.

Approximately 24 percent (five hundred thousand) of the men who served in the Union army and navy were born outside the United States. Even though this means that nearly one of every four soldiers and sailors was an immigrant, foreign-born Americans still were underrepresented as a proportion of the military-age male population. Englishmen and German-born Protestants tended to enlist in numbers larger than their proportion of the population. But Irish- and German-Catholic immigrants seemed generally less eager to volunteer — perhaps because they tended to identify with the Democratic party and associated the war with Republicans. Also, aliens who were not yet citizens and those who arrived to fulfill labor contracts were not liable for the draft. Whatever the cause, the Confederate-proclaimed myth of a Union army composed almost entirely of "foreign hirelings" is precisely that — a myth.

Best estimates of foreign-born Confederate soldiers and sailors conclude that somewhere between 9 and 10 percent of men in the Southern military were immigrants. Yet immigrant men in the South were only 7.5 percent of the total military-age male population. So foreign-born soldiers and sailors were overrepresented in the Confederate military, and assertions that Southern soldiers were all pure, native-born Americans are as false as those that depict Federal armies as foreign hordes.

The contribution of immigrants to the war was indeed significant. During most of the war period, half of the six members of the Confederate cabinet were foreign-born (Judah Benjamin, Christopher Memminger, and Stephen Mallory). And when William Browne was interim secretary of state, two-thirds of the Southern cabinet were immigrants. On the Union side, the navy certainly appreciated the technological innovations of two Swedish natives: Adm. John A. Dahlgren devised the gun named for him that was used widely on Union warships; and John Ericsson developed the *Monitor*, which altered forever naval design and strategy and became the prototype for Federal ironclad vessels. Again on the Confederate side, Dublin-born John Mallet designed vital machinery to make Southern artillery. And Swiss-Southerner Henry Hotze became the Confederacy's foremost propagandist in London. Hotze's newspaper the *Index* printed usually reliable news of the American war and reasoned editorials slanted toward the Confederate cause.

Among those half-million foreign-born troops in the Federal army were six major generals, including Hungarian cavalryman Julius Stahel, who won a Medal of Honor. Twenty brigadier generals were immigrants — born in Germany, Ireland, France, Russia, Hungary, Poland, and Spain. And one of the most renowned Union units was the Irish Brigade from New York.

Of foreign-born Confederate soldiers, two became major generals: French native Camille A. J. M. de Polignac and Irishman Patrick R. Cleburne, the Stonewall of the West. Indeed, it is a safe bet that had it not been for army politics, Cleburne would have become at least a lieutenant general. One Louisiana regiment reportedly counted members from thirty-seven foreign states.

Neither side ever attempted to employ mercenary troops from abroad as the British had done during the Revolution. Nor did European nations intervene in the conflict as many expected. Nevertheless, the American war was a decidedly cosmopolitan affair.

Blacks, like everyone else on the continent, had once been immigrants. But by 1860 the overwhelming majority of them were native-born. The Negro presence and the South's "peculiar institution" that rendered over 3 million Afro-Americans slaves had much to do with the sectional conflict that provoked secession and war. And after Lincoln's Emancipation Proclamation, what had been nominally a war for Union became more clearly also a war against slavery.

One story, perhaps apocryphal, recounts the counsel of an aged black man when younger blacks asked him what they should do about the conflict. Think about this war, the old man said, as a fight between two dogs over a bone. North and South are the dogs, and we are the bone. Did you ever see a dogfight in which the bone took part? Despite the wisdom of the old man's advice, though, Negroes were much involved in the Civil War from its outset.

Although neither side accepted black men as soldiers in 1861, the Federal navy had black sailors from the beginning. Eventually several thousand black men served on Northern vessels. Most prominent was Robert Smalls, who captured the Confederate steamer *Planter* in Charleston harbor and sailed her out to the Federal blockading squadron. Thereafter Smalls served the United States as a pilot for Union warships.

Black men marched off to war with Confederates, too, although they were supposed to be noncombatants. Many Southern officers and some enlisted men took black body servants with them into camp and combat. These men usually performed camp chores for their masters; but in emergency circumstances they were known to take up arms in battle and fight as well. More important to the Southern war effort were the military laborers who toiled within the Confederate military. They dug trenches and fashioned field fortifications, cooked for the troops, and drove wagons and moved supplies to war fronts.

Behind Southern lines black labor was also crucial. The slaves who continued to work on farms and plantations permitted white men to leave those farms and plantations to join

Southern armies without leaving fallow fields. Blacks also worked extensively in the war industries that kept Confederate troops armed and supplied. For example, in the naval ordnance works in Selma, Alabama, 310 of 400 workers were black. And in military hospitals, often more than half of the male nurses were black men.

When Abraham Lincoln delivered the formal, final version of his Emancipation Proclamation on January 1, 1863, he authorized recruitment of black troops in Union armies. Ultimately, an estimated 186,000 black men, 9 percent of the total number of Federal soldiers, literally fought for the cause that freed them.

In several ways, however, the United States tried to make black troops "second-class soldiers." Until late in the war, black men only earned $10.00 per month for their service; the lowest pay for whites was $13.00, plus a $3.50 clothing allowance. Fewer than 100 black men were commissioned combat officers, and none held a rank higher than major. Moreover, the Washington government for a long time resisted committing black regiments to combat and instead used black units for garrison and labor duties. As a result combat deaths among blacks occurred at a rate of about 1.5 percent, compared to 6 percent for whites. The black death rate from disease, however, was 19 percent, nearly double the white rate — facts that reflect the blacks' static service in less than healthy locales.

One reason the Federal War Department shrank from sending black troops into battle was the fear of Southern reprisals against former slaves. In fact the Confederates did threaten to enslave or execute black prisoners, but generally did not carry out such threats. Yet in some cases — most infamously at Fort Pillow, Tennessee, in April 1864, and Saltville, Virginia, that October — Confederates did kill a very high percentage of black Federals, many of whom were already wounded or had surrendered.

When black troops did do battle against the Confederates, they generally acquitted themselves quite well. In Louisiana, at Port Hudson in May 1863 and Milliken's Bend in June, during the campaign for Vicksburg, black regiments earned respect and praise from their white comrades. And had a black division charged first into the Crater at Petersburg in July 1864, as

originally planned, that action might not have been such a bloody Federal fiasco.

As Confederate fortunes and available manpower declined, some Southerners began to favor using black troops. Gen. Patrick Cleburne proposed in writing to the officer corps of the Army of Tennessee in January 1864 that the Confederacy arm and free massive numbers of black men to save the Southern cause. Although Jefferson Davis suppressed Cleburne's paper and the debate that attended it, the idea reappeared during the summer and fall of 1864. Finally Davis asked his congress for an act to arm Southern slaves and free them upon completion of faithful service. The Confederate Congress, after considerable debate throughout the South, authorized black enlistments in mid-March of 1865.

Although a company of black men in gray did drill on Capitol Square in Richmond during the last of March, the Confederate decision to make black men comrades-in-arms came much too late to affect the outcome of the war. Yet on both sides the actions and involvement of Afro-Americans were vital.

By far the largest minority in the United States in 1860, however, were the women — some 48.8 percent of the population. A few women on each side disguised themselves as men and took part in combat. But even though, with a very few exceptions, men did the fighting, women were much involved in the war, both directly and indirectly.

Women served both Union and Confederate armies as spies, and although spying is by nature an extremely secretive activity, some female spies achieved celebrity status for their exploits. Rose O'Neal Greenhow used her social connections in Washington to learn Federal plans for what became the First Manassas campaign and transmitted this intelligence to Confederate general P. G. T. Beauregard. This coup cost Greenhow several months in prison, where she was kept until the spring of 1862, when the Federals sent her south to a heroine's welcome. In the Confederate capital, Elizabeth Van Lew was "Crazy Bet" to her neighbors. But beneath her facade as an eccentric spinster, Van Lew was a Federal spy who organized a circle of Unionists and sent coded messages to Federal generals. Another celebrated Southern spy was Belle Boyd, who escaped arrest to carry vital intelligence to Stonewall Jackson during his Valley campaign. For the Union, Emma E. Edmonds once posed as a black laborer and often disguised herself as a male soldier during the course of numerous daring missions.

On a less elevated plane, wartime generated increased opportunities for some women to practice a much older profession. Extraordinary rates of venereal disease in both armies attest the prevalence of prostitutes and camp followers, who undeniably played a role in meeting some basic needs of the soldiers.

American women began entering, too, what was for them a new profession during the war: they overcame male objections and outright hostility and became nurses. In the North, 3,200 women nursed wounded and diseased soldiers; they constituted about one-fourth of the total number of the Union's nurses. In the South, women quite often responded to medical emergencies with volunteer efforts. But Confederate military hospitals also employed female nurses as official staff members. Mary Walker held a Federal appointment as a surgeon, and Sally Tompkins received a Confederate captain's commission to command a military hospital in Richmond.

Throughout the Union, women responded to the needs of soldiers through the Sanitary Commission. They raised money, purchased or donated food, clothing, and medicine, and distributed these items to the troops. In addition Sanitary Commission volunteers worked with army officers to elevate standards of hygiene and food preparation in military camps. Women in the North also worked through the Christian Commission, an extension of the YMCA, to distribute evangelical tracts and to offer food, care, blankets, and clothing to the troops.

Southern women also formed and assisted volunteer organizations to care for Confederate soldiers. But because the war was often nearby, the women of the Confederacy responded more directly and less institutionally to the needs of the troops. When Confederate units marched through Southern cities and towns, for example, they invariably met sympathetic females who greeted the men with smiles, flowers, and food.

The individual efforts of some wartime women were especially notable. Dorothea Dix served the Union as superintendent of female nurses. She attempted to insure professionalism among her charges by insisting that all of them be over thirty years old and "plain in appearance." Confederate nurse Phoebe Pember gained authority in her ward by seizing the key to the whiskey barrel to control access to the "medicinal spirits." Clara Barton's work with relief agencies during the war enabled her to found the American Red Cross in later years.

Women who remained in their homes, too, quite often felt the impact of the war. For when men went off to fight, the women they left at home of necessity managed the farms, sometimes ran the shops, and usually assumed roles as head of the household. Thus in ways private and subtle, as well as public and obvious, women took part in the war experience.

By 1865 the Civil War had touched individuals and groups of people who seemed immune in 1861. And in turn the total war that Americans fought expanded to encompass issues and aims much larger than the simple question of whether some Southern states could or should secede from the Union. Both in terms of participation and impact, it was everyone's war — a thoroughly national trauma.

It is highly fitting that in a civil war between Americans, the only true native Americans were themselves involved, and just as divided as their white neighbors. Indians fought, often for reasons entirely their own, on both sides. Col. John Drew commanded a regiment of Cherokee Mounted Rifles out west for the Confederacy. (SI)

Richmond sent Brig. Gen. Albert Pike to enlist for the Confederacy the support of the so-called Five Civilized Tribes. He was only partly successful. (NA)

Longtime neighbors—and usually enemies—of the Indians were the
Mexican-Americans living along the border. Many served in both armies,
and those with the Union frequently operated out of Brownsville, Texas,
on the Rio Grande. (USAMHI)

Latin Confederates began their
war service in the command
of Brig. Gen. Henry Hopkins
Sibley, who led them on an ill-
fated campaign to wrest Arizona and
New Mexico from the Union. (USAMHI)

The Thirty-third Texas Cavalry numbered
several Mexican-Americans among its officers,
including Refugio Benavides, at left; Atanacio
Vidaurri, next to him; and Cristobal
Benavides, second from the right. (UAL)

Far more numerous among the soldiers were
the Germans, the largest non-English-
speaking group to enter the war. Fighting
chiefly for the Union, they followed their
own beloved leaders — men like Gen. Franz
Sigel, who, though a miserable leader, could
inspire thousands to enlist. (USAMHI)

Lincoln gave military appointments to many
influential immigrants, chiefly in order to use
their popularity to encourage enlistments.
Carl Schurz, a Prussian revolutionary who
fled Europe for America, became a major
general and — at times — a trusted ally of the
president. (NA)

The Irish, North and South, flocked to their nations' banners in great numbers. Few generals in the Confederate army won a more brilliant reputation than Irish-born Patrick R. Cleburne, sometimes called the Stonewall of the West. He gave his life for the cause at Franklin, Tennessee, in 1864. A previously unpublished portrait. (ADAH)

Across the lines was Brig. Gen. Thomas W. Sweeny, born only a few miles from Cleburne, and pitted against him occasionally in the Atlanta campaign. Something of a professional revolutionary, he tried after the war to foment a revolt against the British in Canada. (NA)

Few units achieved lasting sobriquets, but one of them was the Twenty-third Illinois, which became known to posterity as the Irish Brigade of the West. So potent was the Irish connection that the nickname stuck even though many of its members were not sons of Erin. In 1862 the Irish Brigade wintered at New Creek, in western Virginia. Shown here is their headquarters, "the Den," and standing in front of it, arms folded, is probably their commander, Col. James A. Mulligan. (CHS)

Jews participated in all strata of the war effort, yet ironically it was in the Confederacy, a region notorious for its xenophobia, that a Jew rose the highest. Judah P. Benjamin, a Sephardic Jew born in the West Indies, held three different cabinet posts, most notably secretary of state. (NA)

Adm. John A. Dahlgren, son of a Swedish diplomat to the United States, rose to command the Union's South Atlantic Blockading Squadron, playing a large part in the siege of Charleston and the development of naval weapons. He poses here with the naval deck gun that bears his name. In the distance over his shoulder appear what may be the rubble remains of Fort Sumter. (LC)

Though not foreign-born, Confederate general P. G. T. Beauregard came of French extraction, and rose early in the war to become a Southern hero, and the fifth-highest-ranking officer in the Confederacy. (SHC)

Another Frenchman, this one from Millemont, Seine-et-Oise, was Camille Armand Jules Marie, the Prince de Polignac. Beginning the war on Beauregard's staff, he rose to divisional command. When he died in 1913, he was the last surviving Confederate major general. An unpublished portrait until now. (ADAH)

The Thirty-ninth New York, better known as the Garibaldi Guard, affected not only a resplendent European uniform but also chiefly European officers. Col. Frederick G. D'Utassy commanded. (AIG)

Lt. Col. Alexander Ripetti served with him. (USAMHI)

But largest of all the minorities involved in this war were the people it was all about, the blacks. At first little or no role was expected for them. Pilot Robert Smalls had to make a place in the struggle for himself when . . . (USAMHI)

. . . on May 13, 1862, he seized the steamer *Planter* and sailed her out of Charleston to the hands of the blockading fleet. (NHC)

The only part in the war expected for Southern Negroes was as servants and laborers. Jake Alker spent almost all the war as President Jefferson Davis's manservant. (USAMHI)

When Kentuckian John C. Breckinridge, shown here in 1865 after escaping Federal pursuers, went to war to become a Confederate major general, . . . (WCD)

. . . Tom Ferguson went to war with him as valet. He helped the general make his escape at war's end, and as friends, rather than master and servant, they remained loyal to each other after the conflict ended. (LH)

Young blacks went to war as servants—though not slaves—in the Union army, too. Few officers' messes failed to have at least one "boy" to tease and keep house. (USAMHI)

Many served as cooks and waiters. (JAH)

Some were barely big enough to serve as anything. (USAMHI)

Often they were given cast-off uniforms and allowed to socialize with the men and officers, perhaps earning a few dollars performing odd jobs. (RFC)

A few became regimental mascots, along with dogs and roosters, like these "pets" of the Forty-first Illinois. (TO)

Many able-bodied black men stayed with the armies as paid laborers, digging earthworks, doing the washing, or, as here, helping to clear land and build winter huts. (USAMHI)

For the majority of blacks, the war was an unsettling experience as literally hundreds of thousands of them were uprooted. The refugees and escaped slaves flocked to the armies of the Union wherever they went. These former slaves gathered in New Bern, North Carolina. (USAMHI)

Once the Union government would sanction it, thousands of black men enlisted to fight against the Confederacy, compiling an excellent record despite the handicaps under which they labored. Samuel Cooley photographed this troop of Negro infantrymen in front of the guardhouse at Beaufort, South Carolina, in November 1864. Their officer, standing at far left, is white. (USAMHI)

The First United States Colored Infantry, which saw repeated battle in 1864 and 1865, lost more than seventy in killed and mortally wounded as it became as much a veteran outfit as any white regiment. They stand here at Petersburg in the fall of 1864. (USAMHI)

With only one or two exceptions, no black soldiers rose above this man's rank of sergeant. (JAH)

This sergeant served in the Sixty-second U.S. Colored Infantry in Texas. (JAH)

One of his compatriots in the same regiment. Their unit fought in the actions at Palmito Ranch and White's Ranch, May 12–13, 1865, in Texas. These are generally recognized as being the last engagements of the war. (JAH)

Blacks paid a high price for their participation in the war, especially when facing the hatred of aroused Confederate soldiers. While most wounded and captured black soldiers were treated humanely, occasionally Rebel passions went beyond control. At Fort Pillow, Tennessee, in 1864, scores of wounded and surrendered black soldiers were shot down by cavalrymen led by Gen. Nathan Bedford Forrest. Forrest, shown here in a heretofore unpublished portrait, neither ordered nor condoned the massacre. (ADAH)

Amazingly, as many as two hundred or more women actually managed to pose as soldiers and spend some portion of the war in the field. If she — and her photographer — can be believed, Francis Clalin of Maine became . . . (JAH)

. . . a private in the Thirteenth Maine Cavalry regiment. (JAH)

Women posing as men were generally found out, for there was little place for modesty or privacy in an army. (JAH)

One female corporal was discovered when "he" went into the hospital, and emerged a few days later . . . with a baby. (JAH)

Best known of all the poseurs, and most successful, was Irish-born Jennie Hodgers, shown here at right. She enlisted in the Ninety-fifth Illinois as Albert Cashier, and kept up the sham until 1911 before being discovered. Cashier was a good soldier. (SHW)

Some ladies did not try to fool anyone, but played their part as vivandières, or simply as "mascots" marching with the regiments when home on parade. (JAH)

Others posed as "Miss Liberty" for photographs used to stir patriotism and raise money for soldier relief. (JAH)

North and South, women made their greatest contribution to the war as nurses. Like these ladies at a stove in a hospital tent at City Point, Virginia, they cooked for and otherwise tended the men who had fallen to bullets and disease. (NSHS)

Few of their names are remembered. Harriet Duane was an exception. (USAMHI)

Fewer still were very glamorous, thanks to an edict that nurses ought to be plain, so as not to arouse the soldiers. (USAMHI)

They wrote letters for the wounded and the ill. (USAMHI)

They poured and administered the medicines.
(USAMHI)

In the Confederacy, one of them, Sally
Tompkins, even became the only woman in
the war to hold a military commission. Capt.
Tompkins commanded the Robertson
Hospital in Richmond. (VM)

With the thousands of freedmen gathering around the armies, . . . (USAMHI)

. . . many women went south to act as teachers, bringing education — and a dose of New England religion — to the newly free blacks. (USAMHI)

With the organization of humanitarian groups like the U.S. Sanitary Commission, women found a structured way in which to work for the war effort at home. They raised funds to buy supplies, books, and hire special care for the men in the field, and sent the aid to be administered through agents with the armies. Sanitary Commission headquarters in Richmond at war's end. (USAMHI)

Many of the nurses who followed the armies were hired by the Sanitary Commission, and were themselves members of the group. (USAMHI)

These ladies organized the great New York Sanitary Fair in 1864 as a fund-raising enterprise that proved more than successful. It collected over $1 million for soldier relief. (WRHS)

While the Sanitary Commission tended to the soldiers' physical health, the U.S. Christian Commission sought to care for their spiritual needs, providing thousands of Bibles to the troops from the organization's headquarters in Washington. (USAMHI)

Staffed largely by women, the Christian Commission also employed nurses and maintained offices close to the armies, like this one in Richmond. (USAMHI)

Here at White House Landing, Christian Commission ladies serve coffee to the wounded, cook and wash for them, and serve their other needs, aided by male members of the commission. (NLM)

And whenever they could, loyal and loving wives joined their men in winter quarters to comfort them in ways no nurse or humanitarian could. (USAMHI)

Most often they were the wives of officers who came to spend the idle months with their husbands. (USAMHI)

Regardless of whom they were married to, however, the ladies in camp brought cheer and comfort to all the men, reading to them, helping them with their letters home, and mostly just bringing them a little of the female companionship from home that they were denied. (USAMHI)

For the ladies, as for the men, it was the grandest experience of their generation. (USAMHI)

For all the role that American minorities played, both in bringing on the war and in waging it, nothing could be more fitting than the part played by Seneca sachem Ely S. Parker. Rising high on U. S. Grant's staff, he became a lieutenant colonel and Grant's military secretary. He was one of the few allowed to be with Grant and Lee in their Appomattox interview. And it was Parker who transcribed onto paper Grant's generous terms for surrender. (LC)

The Ravages of War

★ ★

Stephen B. Oates

IT BEGAN with a fanfare of bugles and patriotic oratory, with both sides promising that it would be over in ninety days. From Maine to Texas, volunteers flocked to recruiting centers and marched off to war as young women tossed flowers in their paths. Youths in uniform posed before exploding cameras and sent daguerreotypes of themselves back to their families and sweethearts. They gathered around glowing campfires and spoke in hyperbole about the excitement of battle and what they would do to the enemy when the shooting started. For the volunteers, for civilians in the North and South alike, it was all a picture-book war, a springtime of pomp and pageantry — of fierce drums and blaring bugles, of strutting drum majors and marching bands, of whipping banners and fluttering flags. It was a time when everybody was swept up in the romance of war, in the thrill and dreams of military glory.

What began as a ninety-day lark for both sides swelled instead into a national holocaust, a tornado of blood and wreckage that left scarcely a single family in North or South unscathed. Before it ended, 2.1 million men had gone to war for the Union, nearly 800,000 for the Confederacy. In Dixie, where most of the fighting took place, almost four-fifths of the white men of military age served the Rebel cause, "a *levée en masse*," wrote one historian, "made possible only by the existence of slavery."

There was nothing romantic about this killer war — a brothers' war, the worst kind of human conflict; it released a primordial fury still not understood. How can the cost of the war be reckoned? In numbers alone, the human devastation was staggering. Some 110,000 Federals and 94,000 Confederates lost their lives in combat or from mortal battle wounds. The injured often wished for a merciful bullet, for conditions in Civil War hospitals were ghastly. It was a medically ignorant time; both armies suffered from shortages of doctors and nurses; field hospitals were often pungent barns or chicken coops. In one infirmary a reporter found "the maimed, gashed, and dying" crowded together while a surgeon produced "a little heap of human fingers, feet, legs and arms" wherever he worked. After Gettysburg, Union surgeons consumed five days on amputations — more time than it took to fight the battle. Those who survived combat had to contend with an even deadlier foe: disease. Diarrhea, dysentery, "camp fevers" like malaria and typhoid, and other maladies plagued both armies and claimed more lives than the battles did. On the Union side, diarrhea and dysentery alone killed 44,500 men. In round numbers, some 623,000 American servicemen — 365,000 Federals and 258,000 Confederates — perished in the Civil War. The Union by itself lost more men than the United States did in World War II. Total Civil War casualties almost equaled the combined losses of all of America's other wars.

The fighting in the Civil War was savage beyond computation — a savagery made possible by the most murderous arsenal of destruction Americans had ever assembled. There were the versatile 12-pounder napoleons, the workhorse artillery of both armies, whose canister and grapeshot could obliterate entire lines of advancing infantry. There were the new rifled cannons, macabre guns with flat trajectories and immense hitting power. There were the muzzle-loading Springfield and Enfield rifles, which became the basic infantry weapons for both sides; far more accurate than the smoothbores they replaced, the single-shot rifles had an effective range of four hundred yards and could be loaded and fired three or four times a minute. Add to these the breech-loading repeaters, rudimentary machine guns, and ironclad warships introduced during the conflict, and one understands why experts call it the first modern war in which weapons and machines played a decisive role.

Such weapons turned Civil War battles into human slaughter pens. In one day at Antietam, the bloodiest single day in the annals of American warfare, 2,010 Yankees and 2,700 Rebels were killed and 18,440 combatants were wounded, 3,000 of them mortally. More Americans died that one day than in the War of 1812, the Mexican War, and the Spanish-American War put together. The 12,000 Confederate casualties were double those of U.S. forces on D day.

Losses in the Civil War grew more appalling with every campaign: 23,000 Federals and 28,000 Confederates mowed down or missing at Gettysburg, 64,000 Federals and 32,000 Confederates killed, wounded, or missing in the fighting from the Wilderness to Petersburg in 1864. When ordered to attack entrenched Rebels at Cold Harbor, Virginia, Union troops pinned strips of paper to their coats that gave their names and addresses, so that their bodies could be identified. One doomed Yankee scribbled in his diary: "June 3. Cold Harbor. I was killed." He and 7,000 other Union men were shot dead or wounded in less than an hour of fighting. That was surely the bloodiest hour of combat in all American history.

Gruesome though they are, casualty figures cannot convey what it was like to be in the Civil War. For that we turn to eyewitness accounts, which include some of the most vivid descriptions of the ravages of war ever recorded. Here a Union veteran recalls the horrors of Shiloh:

The ear-piercing and peculiar Rebel yell of the men in gray and answering cheers of the boys in blue rose and fell with the varying tide of battle and, with the hoarse and scarcely distinguishable orders of the officers, the screaming and bursting of shell, the swishing of canister, the roaring of volley firing, the death screams of the stricken and struggling horses and the cries and groans of the wounded formed an indescribable impression which can never be effaced from memory.

A Confederate officer on the Union bombardment of Fredericksburg:

Ten o'clock came, and the hammers of the church clocks were just sounding the last peaceful stroke of the hour, when suddenly, at the signal of a single cannon shot, more then 150 pieces of artillery, including some of the enemy's most ponderous guns, opened their iron mouths with a terrific roar and hurled a tempest of destruction upon the devoted town. The air shook, and the very earth beneath our feet trembled at this deafening cannonade, the heaviest that had ever yet assailed my ears. . . . The howling of the solid shot, the bursting of the shells, the crashing of the missiles through the thick walls and the dull sound of falling houses united in a dismal concert of doom. Very soon the site of the unhappy town was indicated, even through the fog, by a column of smoke and dust and the flames of burning buildings. . . . About noon the sun, breaking through the clouds, seemed to mock the smoking ruins it revealed.

A Union lieutenant on the second day at Gettysburg:

All along the crest everything was ready. Gun after gun, along the batteries, in rapid succession leaped where it stood and bellowed its canister upon the enemy. They still advanced. The infantry opened fire, and soon the whole crest, artillery and infantry, was one continuous sheet of fire. . . . All senses for the time were dead but the one of sight. The roar of the discharges and the yells of the enemy all passed unheeded, but the impassioned soul was all eyes and saw all things that the smoke did not hide. How madly the battery men were driving the double charges of canister into those broad-mouthed Napoleons! How rapidly those long blue-coated lines of infantry delivered their fire down the slope! . . . Men were dropping, dead or wounded, on all sides, by scores and by hundreds. Poor mutilated creatures, some with an arm dangling, some with a leg broken by a bullet, were limping and crawling toward the rear. They made no sound of pain but were as silent as if dumb and mute.

A Union war correspondent on the battlefield the night after Pickett's charge:

I became possessed by a nameless horror. Once I tumbled over two bodies and found my face close to the swollen, bloody features of the man who lay uppermost, judging from the position of other bodies. A shower of grape and canister must have torn the ranks of a regiment into shreds, for 50 or 60 bodies lay there in a row. I came across the corpse of a drummer-boy, his arms still clasped around his drums, his head shattered by a shell. I realized what a price is paid for victories.

Noncombatants paid, too, as the storm uprooted whole communities. Before, during, and after battles, armies of homeless refugees clogged roads and byways. "I never saw a more pitiful procession than they made trudging through the deep snow," a Rebel soldier said of refugees from Fredericksburg.

I saw little children tugging along with their doll babies, holding their feet up carefully above the snow, and women so old and feeble that they could carry nothing and could barely hobble themselves. There were women carrying a baby in one arm and its bottle, clothes and covering in the other. Some had a Bible and a toothbrush in one hand, a picked chicken and a bag of flour in the other. . . . Where they were going we could not tell, and I doubt if they could.

Another class of refugees suffered even more. These were the fugitive slaves, hundreds of thousands of whom abandoned Rebel homesteads and set out for the nearest Union army. In the embattled Mississippi Valley, where fugitives swamped Union lines, an Ohio chaplain wrote that "their condition was appalling. There were men, women and children in every stage of disease or decrepitude, often nearly naked, with flesh torn by the terrible experiences of their escapes." As Sherman's army marched through Georgia, some twenty-five thousand slaves followed it at one time or another — whole families trying to keep pace with the soldiers, with children tied to their parents by a rope. An Indiana officer noted that slave babies "tumbled from the backs of mules to which they had been told to cling, and were drowned in the swamps while mothers stood by the roadside crying for their lost children." Though most of the blacks fell away, too sick or exhausted to continue, seven thousand toiled after Sherman clear to the sea.

It was Sherman, of course, who brought total war to the Deep South, contending as he did that modern wars were won by destroying the enemy's resources as well as his morale. "We are not only fighting hostile armies," Sherman asserted, "but a hostile people, and must make old and young, rich and poor, feel the hard hand of war." That he did, as his army first burned Atlanta — "the workshop of the Confederacy" — while a regimental band played "John Brown's Body." A witness recalled that Yankee soldiers "took up the words wedded to the music, and, high above the roaring flames, above the clash of falling walls, above the fierce crackling of thousands of small-arm cartridges in the burning buildings, rose the triumphant refrain, 'His truth is marching on!'" Then sixty thousand Union troops cut a swath to Savannah 40 miles wide and 220 miles long, visiting war on civilians on a scale unprecedented in America. "We had a gay old campaign," remarked one soldier. "Destroyed all we could eat, stole their niggers, burned their cotton & gins, spilled their sorghum, burned & twisted their R. Roads and raised Hell generally." Sherman estimated the damage at $100 million. Smoldering Georgia was out of the war, her citizens in shock.

Sherman's army now stormed into South Carolina, tearing

up railroads, burning down barns, pulverizing fields of corn and cotton, assassinating cows and chickens, wiping out everything that might sustain dwindling Rebel forces. Civilians fled their homes and evacuated their towns before Sherman's relentless columns. Columbia, the state capital, went up in an inferno of smoke, the conflagration started either by Confederates or Union troops. A Northerner wrote that

most of the citizens of Columbia had sons or relations in the Rebel army. Half of them were dead, and in the blackness of this terrible night their fortunes were all lost. Many wandered about wringing their hands and crying; some sat stolid and speechless in the street, watching everything that they had go to destruction. . . . Most of the people of Columbia would have been willing to die that night, then and there. What had they left to live for? *This, too, was war.*

By now Union forces were smashing up the Confederacy in East and West alike. In the Shenandoah, Philip Sheridan burned a broad path of devastation clear to the Rapidan River. In northwest Alabama, thirteen thousand Union horsemen launched the biggest and most destructive cavalry raid of the war; they crushed their Rebel opponents and burned and wrecked their way clear into southern Georgia. Such scorched-earth warfare earned Lincoln and his generals undying hatred in Dixie, but it brought them victory: within five months after Sherman began his march to the sea, the war was over.

The North suffered terrible human losses, but at least her economy was booming from war production. The South was not only defeated; she was annihilated. Half her men of military age were dead or wounded, two-fifths of her livestock wiped out, more than half her farm machinery demolished, her major cities in ruins, her railroads and industry desolated, her coastal and river ports out of commission, her commerce paralyzed, two-thirds of her assessed wealth, including billions of dollars in slaves, destroyed. "Have we not fallen on sad, sad times?" sighed a Georgia woman as she surveyed the misery around her. Perhaps Southerners now knew what Lincoln had meant when he vowed to teach them "the folly of being the beginners

of war." Perhaps they could all — as a young Texas veteran expressed it — "fall down in the dust and weep over our great misfortune, our great calamities."

Across Dixie the physical damage was everywhere in evidence. Near fire-gutted Columbia, sixty-five horses and mules slain by Sherman's men rotted for six weeks because there were no shovels or other implements with which to bury them. The wreckage in the Tennessee Valley was typical of the dead Confederacy. Here an English traveler found "plantations of which the ruin is for the present total and complete," and a trail of war visible "in burnt up gin houses, ruined bridges, mills, and factories." He added, in reference to the vanquished slave-owning class, that "many who were the richest men . . . have disappeared from the scene."

Few Southerners were more destitute than the former slaves. Owning little more than the skin on their backs, they streamed by the thousands into Union army bivouacs or the nearest towns and cities. The Freedmen's Bureau set up relief camps and throughout the summer of 1865 distributed 100,000 daily rations to suffering blacks. But the camps were so crowded that epidemics killed a third of the people in them.

Whites were scarcely better off, as roving bands of thieves pillaged defenseless homes and famine and disease plagued the land. An official of the Freedmen's Bureau reported as "an everyday sight" women and children "begging for bread from door to door." The bureau gave out thousands of daily rations to whites too (total rations to whites and blacks came to 22 million between 1865 and 1870). Into "the vacuum of chaos and destruction," as one writer phrased it, came 200,000 occupation troops, who managed to restore some semblance of order to war-ravaged Dixie.

How much did the war cost both sections? Exact figures are hard to come by, especially for the Confederacy. Surviving records indicate that by October 1863 Confederate war expenditures had exceeded $2 billion. By 1879, according to one estimate, Union expenses growing out of the war were more than $6 billion. But these sums excluded the war debts of the states. Adding up estimates of those debts, Union and Confederate war expenses, total property loss, federal pensions to 1917, and interest to the national debt, one historian put the overall cost of the war at about $20 billion.

But this does not count the billions of dollars it took to rebuild the South. Nor does it include losses from reduced Southern production. The South's economy was so crippled that her per-capita output did not return to the antebellum level for more than fifty years after Appomattox. The South's per-capita income, 33 percent lower than the North's in 1860, was 40 percent lower in 1880 and stayed there until the twentieth century.

But dollars and percentages cannot gauge the full toll of the Civil War. One must look at the photographs to comprehend what it did to the land and the cities: the rubble of Richmond . . . the burned-out Gallego Flour Mills there . . . the fields of skull and bone . . . the maimed bodies of the wounded . . . the face of exhaustion in the North . . . the visage of defeat in Dixie.

But not even the photographs capture the emotional and psychological scars left by the conflict. Who knows what damage it did to the American spirit? Who can measure the mental anguish and human suffering that continued long after the guns were silent? Who can say how deep the bitterness and humiliation ran in the South, where millions of unrepentant whites embraced the legend of the lost cause and forged a bastion of white supremacy that lasted a century?

In time, though, some of the bitterness faded with the battle flags, and hard-bitten veterans of both armies, many with arms and legs gone, with eyes shot out and faces disfigured, marched in memorial parades and wept at speeches of remembered valor. And so in the veterans' reunions the war ended as it had begun — in an aura of glory.

But beyond the parades and reunions were grim reminders of what really happened in that war. There were the cemeteries in both sections, quiet fields where soldiers lay in ranks of white gravestones. There were the battlefield parks, with their polished cannons and statues of singular men frozen in marble. Here, if he listens closely, the visitor today can hear the echoes of the war — the rattle of musketry, the deadly whir of grapeshot, the ring of sabers, the shouts. He can almost see colliding lines of infantry and shell-torn flags in the smoke, can almost smell the acrid odor of gunpowder and the stench of death on the wind. The battlefields recall what madness beset Americans from 1861 to 1865 and what the nation paid, and paid dearly, for its survival. At every battle site there ought to be a shrine to those broken and bloodied men, with the inscription "Lord God of hosts, Be with us yet, Lest we forget, Lest we forget. . . ."

No words could ever tell this Confederate boy what he gave up for his country. (USAMHI)

Yet sometimes the dead were the fortunate ones. For the wounded, like these Yanks
in bandages and slings at Savage Station, Virginia, awaiting transport to hospitals, the
real nightmare might lay ahead. Chances are that many an arm and leg, and life, in
this image did not long survive. (CHS)

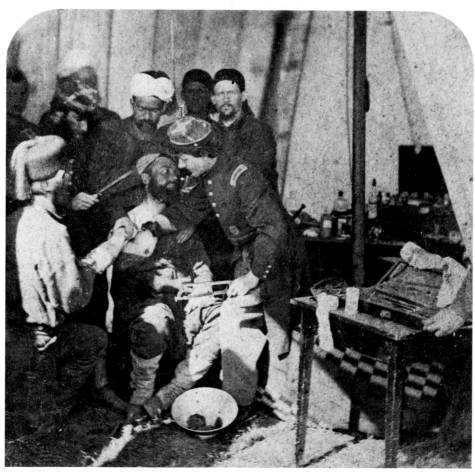

For all too many, alas, the surgeon's knife
awaited. The Yank in this surgeon's hands at
Fort Monroe is lucky: he is only posing in a
mock scene. One bullet could put him in
that surgeon's chair in extremis. (UR)

This field surgeon's tent looks more like
what most wounded Yanks first saw, with its
sign warning of "No Admittance except by
permission of the Surgeon." But the chaos of
battlefield surgery is still nowhere evident in
this posed image. (JAH)

Top left: Their medicines were rudimentary, and their training often no better. (JAH)

Top right: For Confederate medicos like surgeon Watson M. Gentry, conditions were even worse when the war and blockade made medicines scarce. It was the soldiers themselves who inevitably suffered the most. (MC)

Suffer they did. This boy will lose his gangrenous foot. (AFIP)

Top left: This youthful sergeant of the Sixteenth Pennsylvania may keep his arm, with luck. (RP)

Top right: The bullets paid little heed to rank. High and low alike could suffer. Brig. Gen. Henry A. Barnum suffered wounds three times in the war, and delighted in posing to display this one in particular — sometimes with a leather strap, here with a string, drawn clear through his body. (AFIP)

Bottom left: Generals on the other side felt the same sting of lead. Brig. Gen. Adam R. Johnson was shot accidentally by his own men in a mishap that almost completely destroyed his eyes, leaving him virtually blind. (WCD)

As the war ravaged landscape and inhabitants alike, more and more space had to be commandeered to house the wounded and recovering. Cities like Memphis became virtual hospital metropolises. This building may have been a stove works, judging from the small parlor stove atop the post at right. Here it has become Webster U.S. Military General Hospital. (CHB)

Memphis confectioners made candy here until the war transformed the factory into the Washington U.S. Military General Hospital. The only thing sweet at this point was getting out alive. (CHB)

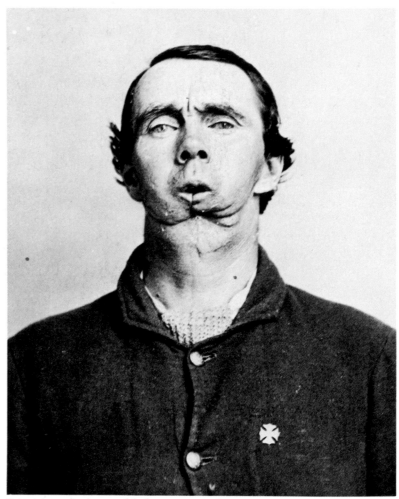

And all too often, those who lived through their wounds did so with grim prospects for the future. (AFIP)

Primitive surgery could close a wound. Nothing of the time would replace a jaw shot away. (AFIP)

Top left: Streets North and South were full of empty sleeves after the war. (JAH)

Top right: A blindfold could hide the ravages of lost eyes, but not a lost future. (JAH)

Inventive minds could equip this poor Yank with fork and spoon. He could feed himself. But his hands would never feel the softness of a woman's hair or the velvet of his child's cheek. (BA)

Behind the living lay the dead, scattered all across the continent. They covered the fields, like these Johnny Rebs at Antietam. (USAMHI)

And like these Confederates sprawled in death at Gettysburg. (LC)

For those not touched by war's bullets, still there was the dislocation suffered by hundreds of thousands — especially the slaves. Escape from their owners and freedom were wonderful things. But who would feed them now, and where would they live and work? Freedmen at Petersburg late in the war. (CHS)

Until they could take care of themselves and be relocated, they were virtual wards of the Union, dependent, like these freedmen in South Carolina, for the rations being issued them and the clothes on their backs. (USAMHI)

And how the land itself had been ravaged by
the passing armies. (USAMHI)

Everywhere was disruption and destruction,
as here at Fort Moultrie. (USAMHI)

Towns like Donaldsonville, Louisiana, lay in ruins. (ISHL)

The pitiful little industry of places like Port
Hudson sat destroyed. (USAMHI)

Two years after the war, the craters and trenches and earthworks still scarred the land around Petersburg. (LAW)

Bottom left: Light would never shine forth again from South Carolina's Beacon House. (USAMHI)

Bottom right: Nothing but charred chimneys remained to remind of the once-beautiful homes that fell victim to the fires of war. (USAMHI)

The lovely and stately Fauquier Springs Hotel . . . (USAMHI)

. . . was now only a stately ruin. (USAMHI)

Major cities like Atlanta sat
ravaged. (LC)

South Carolina's capital city, Columbia, was virtually laid waste. Months after the war, when George Barnard's camera came, the rubble of the capitol lay where it had fallen in the fires. (LC)

Of the South's major cities, only a few survived unscathed — notably, Savannah. (KA)

Not so Charleston, cradle of the Confederacy. Four years of intermittent siege left much of the city in ruins. (USAMHI)

Its once-thriving city market at right barely survived the conflagration that claimed
the block across the street. (USAMHI)

Secession Hall, where South Carolinians voted to leave the Union and thus precipitated the sections on the road to war, was left as nothing but a crumbling wall. (USAMHI)

The famous Circular Church next door, though severely mauled, would survive, to begin restoration almost at once. (USAMHI)

The task facing Charlestonians was awesome.
(USAMHI)

As with the nation itself, the work of
rebuilding would take years, and some scars
would always show. (USAMHI)

Of some once-treasured buildings, there was
nothing left to rebuild. (USAMHI)

Broad Street once thrived. Now it looked
like a Roman ruin. (USAMHI)

The houses of the Almighty were not spared from the conflagration. (USAMHI)

Doors that once opened to the faithful now lay open to the elements. (USAMHI)

Halls that echoed to the sound of voices raised in praise now heard only the howling of the winds. (USAMHI)

Charlestonians almost lost their hearts with their city. (USAMHI)

Worse, besides the destruction of shot and shell, the city had suffered an accidental fire in 1861 that ravaged much — as if even chance had conspired against the once-beautiful Southern metropolis. (USAMHI)

The flames knew no denomination, no politics. (USAMHI)

Some in the North would claim that the secession virus could only be eradicated by flames. (USAMHI)

If so, then surely by 1865 Charleston must have been cleansed. (USAMHI)

Miraculously, the city's orphan asylum was largely spared. (USAMHI)

But not so the graves of Charlestonians long gone, in the churchyard at the Circular Church. (USAMHI)

The Northeastern Railroad Depot lay in rubble. (USAMHI)

And the Battery, once the most beautiful seaside promenade in the South, saw many of the finest homes in America shattered. Charleston had paid dearly for her experiment in rebellion. (USAMHI)

Top left: The destruction spread everywhere the armies went. To the homes . . . (USAMHI)

Top right: . . . and backyards of Petersburg, . . . (USAMHI)

Bottom right: . . . and most of all to Richmond. The Virginia State House in the background, itself spared the conflagration, surveys a scene of unimagincd ruin. (USAMHI)

On April 6 in Richmond, four days after the city's evacuation, Alexander Gardner found a vista of devastation wherever he pointed his camera. (USAMHI)

All that remained of the Richmond & Petersburg Railroad bridge over the James was its northernmost arch. The Franklin Paper Mill behind it was nothing but a hollow shell. (USAMHI)

Looking across the James from the South, the bridge piers rose starkly out of the river, pointing the way to the ruins of the city beyond. (USAMHI)

A cameraman could use the last arch of the bridge to frame a portrait of war's ravages. (USAMHI)

Whole blocks on Cary Street simply ceased to be. (USAMHI)

Richmond had become a city of brick skeletons. (USAMHI)

So traumatic was the fire that wasted the city on April 2, 1865, and the days following, that forever afterward Richmonders would refer to this one portion of their city simply as the "burnt district." (USAMHI)

To the camera's eye, it was a dead city. (USAMHI)

Its inhabitants were the ghosts of places that once teemed with the life of a capital at war. (USAMHI)

Its banks, like the Exchange, had nothing in their vaults now but dust. (USAMHI)

The rails were burned out from under the engines at the Richmond & Petersburg depot. (USAMHI)

Tredegar Iron Works, like its city and its
cause, was dead. (USAMHI)

Richmond, like the South itself, looked as if
it might never again rise from its ruins.
Such was the havoc of war. (USAMHI)

These Gallego Flour Mills, photographed by Gardner that April, once produced twenty-four hundred barrels of flour a day. (USAMHI)

Now they would produce only brick to be salvaged for the rebuilding of the city. (USAMHI)

Hardest of all were the human costs, North and South. For years afterward, the soil of Virginia and Tennessee and a dozen other states would sprout this bitter crop after the spring rains. (USAMHI)

Enriching that soil was the lifeblood of the
nations' youth. Bright-eyed boys had gone off
to war. (FS)

Some, like these cadets of the Virginia
Military Institute, actually prayed that the
war would last long enough for them to be
of age to fight. (VM)

For those not killed or wounded, there were still other perils to face, still more ravages awaiting. These Confederates are the surrendered garrison of Port Hudson. Ahead of them lay prison camps, and hardship and disease such as Americans at war had never before experienced. (ISHL)

Over 400,000 men in blue and gray went to prison camps. Better than 56,000 of them died there. Some 12 percent of these Rebels awaiting shipment north at Belle Plain, Virginia, in May 1864, would die in captivity. (USAMHI)

It was worse for Federals sent to Southern prison camps, thanks in part to the scarcity that plagued the Confederates and in part to the failures of Brig. Gen. John Winder, commissary general of prisoners. Unjustly accused of starving Yankee prisoners to death, he would likely have been tried and executed for war crimes had he not died shortly before the surrender. (SHC)

The infamous prisons appeared all over the country. Some, like the Texas State Penitentiary at Huntsville, were already standing. (USAMHI)

Others, like Belle Isle, in the middle of the James opposite Richmond, were hastily appropriated to house captured Federals. This image by the Confederate photographer David R. Rees shows the tents that gave Yankee prisoners rude shelter in 1863. (VM)

Rees also photographed a far more infamous Richmond bastille, Libby Prison. Once a ship chandlery, it became home for thousands of Union officers. (USAMHI)

The interior of Libby was stark, plain, and fatally overcrowded. (CHS)

In this room Union colonel Abel D. Streight was kept along with several hundred others. (CHS)

Top right: Most notorious of all, of course, was Camp Sumter in Georgia, known forever as Andersonville. Confederate cameraman A. J. Riddle photographed it on August 17, 1864, already crammed with some of the 33,000 men who packed its twenty-six acres that summer. (USAMHI)

Bottom left: They seemed literally to be living in standing room only. (USAMHI)

Bottom right: The few officers incarcerated at Camp Sumter had their own private pen — nothing more than a small stockade — photographed here just after the war by Engle & Furlong of Fernandina, Florida. (NA)

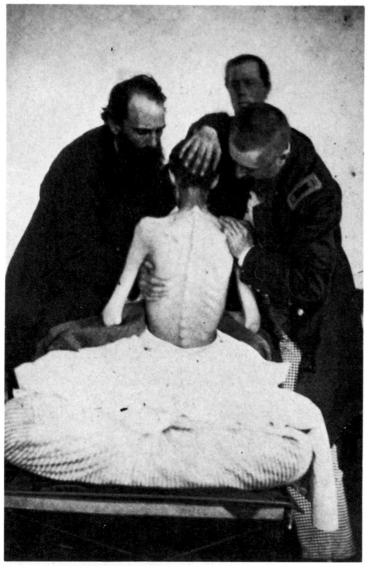

Thousands died. Of those who survived, many looked like the living dead. Pvt. Isaiah Bowker was released from Belle Isle in March 1864 and lived but two months. (USAMHI)

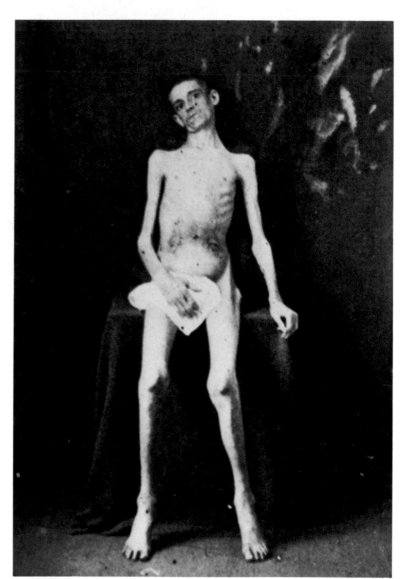

Pvt. William M. Smith was released two months after Bowker, little more than a skeleton. He would live. (USAMHI)

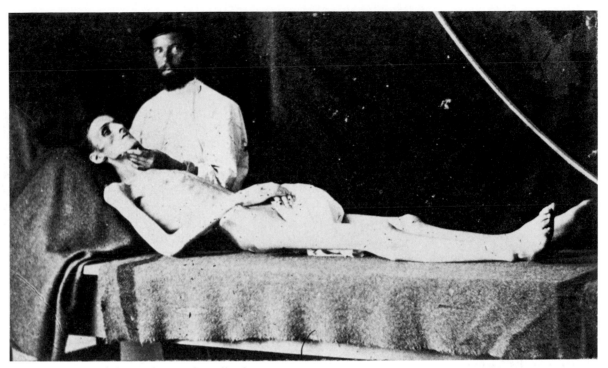

Pvt. John Rose of Kentucky was literally skin
and bones upon his release. (USAMHI)

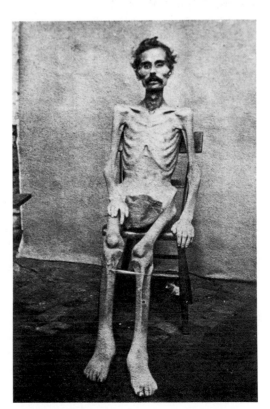

While released Confederate prisoners seem
not to have been photographed like their
Yankee counterparts, many of them would
have looked no better than this freed Union
soldier. Overcrowding, disease, poor sanitation, and inadequate food made prison life
hell without regard for a soldier's politics.
(USAMHI)

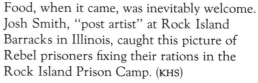

Food, when it came, was inevitably welcome. Josh Smith, "post artist" at Rock Island Barracks in Illinois, caught this picture of Rebel prisoners fixing their rations in the Rock Island Prison Camp. (KHS)

Hungry, lonely, far from home and perhaps even afraid, men of both sides would still sit for the camera—like these Johnny Rebs in Camp Chase Prison, in Ohio, sitting for M. M. Griswold. If they could pose, at least they were still alive. (RP)

The war had left so many others unable to pose ever again. The cemeteries North and South burgeoned with the dead. They were in vaults in the French cemetery in New Orleans. (USAMHI)

They were laid in a grassy plot called Hollywood Cemetery overlooking the James in Richmond. (USAMHI)

Many remained on the battlefields where they fell, their names scrawled on rude headboards like these near Bull Run. (USAMHI)

Some were remembered more permanently. These Billy Yanks died in the struggle for the Mississippi, and lie buried near Baton Rouge. (USAMHI)

Alas, the tragedy of death did not even end with the cessation of hostilities. On April 26, 1865, with all but one of the Confederate armies surrendered and the war virtually done, photographer T. W. Bankes of Helena, Arkansas, took his camera to the wharf on the Mississippi and took this image of the steamer *Sultana*, crowded with 2,021 men, most of them released prisoners from Rebel camps farther south. They were on the way home. The next morning, before dawn, the ship exploded, burned, and sank. Estimates of the dead range from 1,238 to over 1,900—one of the worst ship losses in history. (SBS)

For the Rebels, there remained ahead years of living in humiliation as an occupied land. To maintain the peace and ensure that the South accepted the verdict of the war, Federal soldiers would be stationed in the former Confederacy for twelve years after the surrender. Their barracks, like these on the grounds of Atlanta's city hall, were a constant reminder of defeat. (LC)

And all across America there were other reminders of the ravages of war — among them buildings like this simple house in Gettysburg, where once the armies fought the greatest battle of the war. Now it served the ends of peace, as a school to educate the orphaned children of the men who went off to war, never to return. (USAMHI)

The War to Posterity

A portfolio of images capturing the
continuing impact and dwindling vestiges
of the greatest epic in American history

In May 1865, Maj. Gen. John Gibbon was ordered to take the captured and surrendered
battle flags of Lee's army to Washington after the capitulation at Appomattox. Gibbon
took with him some of the brave men who had performed special feats in capturing
those flags, and here he posed with them and their flags for Alexander Gardner's
camera. Gibbon himself stands, thumb in belt, directly in front of the tree at left. (AIG)

The vicious contest done, the commemoration, more an expression of relief than of exultation, began. First, and most appropriate, it came here in the savaged parade ground of Fort Sumter. (USAMHI)

Amid the rubble, the shot, and dismounted cannons, the conquering Federals erected seats. (USAMHI)

Top right: A makeshift pavilion went up in the center. (USAMHI)

Bottom left: Flags and bunting draped the frame. (USAMHI)

Bottom right: And on April 14, 1865, the fourth anniversary of Sumter's fall, Major — now General — Robert Anderson and a host of dignitaries gathered to raise once more the flag of the Union over the pile of rubble. (USAMHI)

Already the monuments began to sprout from the ground. Out in Mississippi, where Gen. John C. Pemberton met with Grant to surrender the Vicksburg garrison in 1863, a simple marker appeared to memorialize the surrender site. Cannons that once spat fire and shell at men now pointed skyward in peace. (USAMHI)

On the fields near Manassas, Virginia, veterans erected this simple monument "In Memory of the Patriots Who Fell at Bull Run, July 21st, 1861." (USAMHI)

Soldiers erected it in June 1865 — one of the most unassuming monuments the war would inspire. Within a few weeks, some local birds found it so unassuming that they built a nest atop the pyramid. (USAMHI)

Soldiers returned to some of the battlefields while the smoke of war seemed still to linger. Hospitals and cemeteries were established on some. Here at Gettysburg in July 1865, some Federals have come back already to work on the Soldiers' National Monument. (USAMHI)

First among the monuments were those built to honor the dead. In the new Arlington National Cemetery, 2,111 of the unknown dead from Virginia's battlefields were put to rest in 1866 beneath this memorial. (USAMHI)

All across the country, in family plots and churchyards, the granite and marble markers remembered the dead. Lt. Charles H. Swasey, killed aboard his ship in 1862, lies here now at rest in Taunton, Massachusetts. (USAMHI)

And the monuments went up for those who did not die in the conflict, but who helped guide it and yet did not long survive. Lt. Gen. Winfield Scott survived the war by only a year. They laid him to rest at West Point. (USAMHI)

Fields of granite sprouted all over the reunited states. Some twelve thousand of these fifteen thousand graves at Arlington mark the unknown. (USAMHI)

In row upon endless row they lie, in forma-
tions more straight than any the simple
farmers and clerks maintained in life. "The
hopes, the tears, the blood, that marked the
bitter strife," reads the sign, "are now all
crowned by Victory, that saved the Nation's
life." (USAMHI)

Soon the more prosperous Northern
veterans, backed by their state legislatures,
began to put up monuments in the South
where their sons had fallen. Massachusetts
usually led the way, as with this soldiers and
sailors' monument for those who fell in
North Carolina. (USAMHI)

Confederate survivors, often struggling just to live, could ill afford much in the early years after the war. This simple marker at Shepherdstown, West Virginia, was the first such erected in the South. (USAMHI)

In time the South, too, would afford more imposing monuments — and it, too, had its share of unknowns to honor. (USAMHI)

Some of the known Confederate dead would always receive special remembrance, and few more so than the fallen general J. E. B. Stuart, whose grave in Richmond's Hollywood Cemetery was almost a shrine to one who was dead "yet immortal." (KHS)

The leaders who survived went on into the peacetime world, covered with their honors, able now to devote some of their energies to the pursuits of peace. Gen. U. S. Grant, standing with hand in pocket at center, and Adm. David G. Farragut, standing at far left, could turn philanthropist as trustees of the Peabody Fund, which was sponsored by George Peabody, seated at left, to promote education in the South. (USAMHI)

Others, however, saw little ahead for them in the years after the war. The so-called Wild West was a direct offspring of the Civil War. Thousands of deserters, refugees, guerrillas, and others too used to lawlessness to reform crossed the Mississippi to the frontier. Men like these rugged westerners of Terry's Texas Rangers furnished the raw materials of both outlaws and peacekeepers. (PPHM)

There were wild years ahead for many. The war of expansion that had been waged against the American Indian for two centuries before secession continued toward its inevitable conclusion, with only occasional setbacks. None so shocked the nation as the defeat at the Little Bighorn in Montana in 1876. Heading the list of names of the dead on the Seventh Cavalry monument was its commander, George A. Custer. (USAMHI)

And within a couple of decades after the war, age and death began to claim all its surviving leaders. Nathaniel Banks had been a failure as a general, but Waltham, Massachusetts, gave his mortal remains a hero's farewell. (USAMHI)

Gen. James Longstreet, Lee's old war-horse, lost the respect of many former Confederates when he spoke critically of Lee after the war and became a Republican. But when he died in 1904, much was forgiven, and throngs of Southerners joined in his funeral procession. (USAMHI)

He was the last of the high-ranking Rebel generals, and they buried him in Gainesville, Georgia, as if he had been a Viking chieftain of old. (USAMHI)

One week after Longstreet's death, another Confederate giant passed away.
Maj. Gen. John B. Gordon of Georgia was one of the premier organizers of the
Confederate veterans after the war, and served as the first commander of their
national veterans' organization. His funeral in Atlanta was a solemn occasion. (USAMHI)

Old veterans clad in gray bore his flag-draped coffin. (USAMHI)

The old and young alike stood reverently over his flower-strewn graveside. As the old soldiers were dying, only the memory of what they had done lived on. (USAMHI)

The Union, too, lost her heroes — none greater than Grant. Dying of throat cancer, he finished his memoirs in 1885, just days before his death. (USAMHI)

Bottom left: A far cry from the hardscrabble surroundings of his youth, this parlor in his summer home in Mount McGregor, New York, is where Grant spent his last days. (USAMHI)

Bottom right: And this is the sickroom in which he fought his battle with cancer and time. (USAMHI)

When Grant died, the whole nation mourned. For miles along its length, New York's Broadway stood packed for his funeral procession. (USAMHI)

Even old enemies like the Virginians in this heavily retouched photograph, men of the old Stonewall Brigade, came to march and pay respect to one who had been magnanimous in victory. (USAMHI)

"The World Has Lost a Hero," proclaims a banner raised by Austrians watching the funeral. Grant's portraits lined the streets as the extravagance of his funeral marked a stark contrast with the humble beginnings of the Union's first soldier. (USAMHI)

Upon his tomb the honors were laid as the nation bade him farewell, his postwar failures forgotten in the surge of nostalgic reverie over his wartime achievements. (USAMHI)

With the soldiers dying rapidly as the years wore on, Americans treasured the more lasting relics of the great war. As early as 1866, Clara Barton displayed and sold souvenirs of the hellhole at Andersonville to raise money for veteran relief. (USAMHI)

Other relics were preserved with more honored recollections, reminders of heroism and sacrifice. The Western & Atlantic Railroad engine *General* was kept in the Chattanooga station to recall the epic story of its theft and recovery in the daring 1862 "Great Locomotive Chase." (USAMHI)

Most lasting of all, of course, were the battlefields themselves. From the day the war ended, work began to preserve and mark them for posterity. By the turn of the century, Gettysburg was already the best-memorialized battlefield in the world. (USAMHI)

Distinguished visitors came to see where the victories and defeats of old had happened. President William H. Taft had been a mere child when the war began. In May 1909, within months after his inauguration, he came to Gettysburg to survey the field. Here, he sits at far left in the back of the automobile as it passes before the equestrian statue of Gen. John F. Reynolds. (USAMHI)

As the years went on, so did the work of
erecting more and more monuments to
commemorate the past. The huge chunks of
granite were common sights on the roads of
America. (USAMHI)

And so were the ceremonies after the stone
and bronze had been joined. (USAMHI)

The great cities dedicated squares and parks to their heroes. In Boston, men remove their hats as a crowd assembled at the State House eagerly waits for the flag and fabric veiling a statue to come down, . . . (USAMHI)

. . . revealing an equestrian of Maj. Gen. Joseph Hooker. Cameramen record the scene as musicians and dignitaries crane their necks and the audience applauds. The North would be in its glory for decades after the victory. (USAMHI)

Top left: They had all, North and South, come a long way from those old war days when men like Joslyn & Smith of the Washington Photograph Gallery in Vicksburg captured the image of the war that so changed them all. (JAH)

Top right: Like Royan Linn, who kept his camera in a shed atop Lookout Mountain in Tennessee, they had a sense of history, of the meaning of what they had endured. (JAH)

Like the scores of photographers whose vans and wagons had followed the armies in the days of 1861–1865, they knew they had been a part of something special, for all its horrors. (USAMHI)

Many of the scenes of former glory were overgrown and lost, like Fort Bartow near Savannah. (USAMHI)

Nature reclaimed much that had been her own in days before the war — such as this powder magazine on Green Island, Georgia. (USAMHI)

But the memories of the men would last forever. They began to gather soon after the war itself was done. Men of John Hunt Morgan's Kentucky Confederate Cavalry met in reunion in the Ashland woods in Lexington in 1867, and would do so again and again. (KHS)

Old veterans of the Forty-first Georgia gathered in 1880 to talk of their old times. (WA)

At Gettysburg in 1913, thousands of veterans of both sides met for a fiftieth reunion — Johnny Reb and Billy Yank sitting side by side in comradeship. (LC)

The years took their toll. As time went on, there were fewer and fewer. At the annual Confederate Veterans reunion in Richmond in 1922, the numbers of Johnny Rebs had dwindled drastically. (WA)

Many of their comrades were so invalided as to be confined to the soldiers' homes like this one in Richmond, there to so end their last days with fellow soldiers, reliving in memory the days of old. (USAMHI)

They brought out proudly their holy relics. Col. D. H. Lee Martz, at left, displays the battle flag of his old regiment, the Tenth Virginia. (USAMHI)

At last, North and South, there came a time
when the veterans were no more. The last
Confederate reunion took place in Richmond
in June 1951. These three fading soldiers,
each well over one hundred, were all that was
left. Before the decade was out, they would
all be gone. (WA)

The battle flag of the Sixteenth Confederate
Cavalry flew over one of the last Rebel battle
lines, at Whistler, Alabama, in April 1865.
Silas Buck carried it then, and fifty years
later he still stood proudly with the old
banner. (KHS)

Behind them they left an indelible record of bravery and sacrifice. Behind them were the three million Rebs and Yanks who had fought and gone before them. Behind them they, like the nation of which they were all a part, left their innocence . . . and their youth. (WA)

Contributors

HAROLD M. HYMAN is one of the most distinguished historians of the Civil War, noted especially for his work on the legal and constitutional aspects of the conflict. For many years a professor of history at Houston's Rice University, he has authored highly acclaimed works on Union oaths and loyalty tests, and the definitive biography of Edwin M. Stanton.

MAURY KLEIN, Professor of History at the University of Rhode Island, is the author of a number of outstanding books, including a biography of Gen. E. Porter Alexander, a history of the Louisville & Nashville Railroad, and a forthcoming biography of financier Jay Gould.

ROBERT K. KRICK is Historian at the Fredericksburg-Spotsylvania National Military Park, and one of the leading students of the Army of Northern Virginia. In addition, he has compiled noted bibliographies of Civil War literature, and has authored several books, including regimental histories of Virginia units, and *Lee's Colonels*, a biographical directory of field officers who served in the Army of Northern Virginia.

STEPHEN B. OATES is one of America's most noted and popular biographers, the author of acclaimed biographies of Abraham Lincoln, John Brown, Nat Turner, Martin Luther King, Jr., and a forthcoming work on William Faulkner. Professor of History at the University of Massachusetts at Amherst, he conducts special courses and symposia on the art of biography.

EMORY M. THOMAS of the University of Georgia has achieved an enviable reputation as a Civil War historian. His most recent work, a biography of the Confederate general J. E. B. Stuart, follows a series of distinguished works on Richmond during the war, the Confederacy as a revolutionary experience, and a one-volume history of the Confederate nation.

WILLIAM C. DAVIS, Editor of this work, is the author or editor of twenty books dealing with the Civil War and Southern history, including the six-volume *Image of War* photographic series. In recognition for this last work, he was in 1985 elected a Fellow of the Royal Photographic Society of Bath, England. For many years editor of the magazine *Civil War Times Illustrated*, he now divides his time between writing and publishing.

WILLIAM A. FRASSANITO, Photographic Consultant for *Touched by Fire*, is the country's foremost Civil War photographic historian, having elevated the study of the old images from an antiquarian interest to a serious historical discipline. The author of a brilliant trilogy dealing with the images of Antietam, Gettysburg, and the 1864–65 campaign in Virginia, he resides in Gettysburg, where he continues his studies into the Civil War and its images.

Photograph Credits

Abbreviations accompanying each image indicate the contributor. Full citations appear below. Very grateful acknowledgment is extended to the individuals and institutions, both public and private, who have so generously allowed the use of their priceless photographs.

ADAH	Alabama Department of Archives and History, Montgomery
AFIP	Armed Forces Institute of Pathology, Washington, D.C.
AIG	Americana Image Gallery, Gettysburg, Pa.
ARCM	Augusta-Richmond County Museum, Augusta, Ga.
BA	Burns Archive Historic Medical Photographs
BHC	Burton Historical Collection, Detroit Public Library
BPL	Bridgeport Public Library, Bridgeport, Conn.
CHB	Charles H. Bournstine
CHS	Chicago Historical Society
CWTIC	*Civil War Times Illustrated* Collection, Harrisburg, Pa.
DWM	Drake Well Museum, Titusville, Pa.
FL	Frederick Lightfoot
FS	Fred Slaton
GDAH	Georgia Department of Archives and History, Atlanta
HEHL	Henry E. Huntington Library, San Marino, Calif.
HLY	Harold L. Yazel
HP	Herb Peck, Jr.
ISHL	Illinois State Historical Library, Springfield
JAH	John A. Hess
JCF	James C. Frasca
KA	Kean Archives, Philadelphia
KHS	Kentucky Historical Society, Frankfort
KKCPL	Knoxville–Knox County Public Library, Knoxville, Tenn.
LAW	Lee A. Wallace, Jr.
LAWLM	Louis A. Warren Library and Museum, Fort Wayne, Ind.
LC	Library of Congress, Washington, D.C.
LCP	Library Company of Philadelphia
LH	Louisa Hill
LO	Lloyd Ostendorf
MC	Museum of the Confederacy, Richmond, Va.
MDSSA	Michigan Department of State, State Archives, Lansing
MHC	Michigan Historical Collection, Bentley Historical Library, University of Michigan, Ann Arbor
NA	National Archives, Washington, D.C.
NCDAH	North Carolina Department of Archives and History, Raleigh
NHC	Naval Historical Center, Washington, D.C.
NLM	National Library of Medicine, Bethesda, Md.
NSHS	Nebraska State Historical Society, Lincoln
NYHS	New-York Historical Society, New York City
PPHM	Panhandle-Plains Historical Museum, Canyon, Tex.
RFC	Richard F. Carlile
RP	Ronn Palm
SBS	Stephen B. Smith
SHC	Southern Historical Collection, University of North Carolina, Chapel Hill
SHW	Spencer H. Watterson
SI	Smithsonian Institution, Washington, D.C.
SRF	Seventh Regiment Fund, Inc., New York City (copied by Al Freni)
TF	Thomas Ferguson, Springfield, Mo.
TO	Terence O'Leary
TPS	Thomas P. Sweeney, M.D., Springfield, Mo.
TU	Tulane University, New Orleans
UAL	Ursuline Academy Library, San Antonio, Tex.
UR	University of Rochester, Rochester, N.Y.
USAMHI	U.S. Army Military History Institute, Carlisle Barracks, Pa.
VHS	Vermont Historical Society, Montpelier
VM	Valentine Museum, Richmond, Va.
WA	William Albaugh
WAF	William A. Frassanito
WCD	William C. Davis
WCHS	Washington County Historical Society, Fayetteville, Ark.
WMA	William M. Anderson
WRHS	Western Reserve Historical Society, Cleveland
WVU	West Virginia University, Morgantown

Index

Page numbers in *italics* denote photographs of the subject.

agriculture, 41–43, 74
Aiken's Landing, Va., 72
Alexander, E. P., 115, 116
Alexandria, Va., *59, 67, 70,* 165
Alker, Jake, *215*
ambulance yard, *99*
American Red Cross, 205
Anderson, Robert, *135,* 140, 299
Andersonville, Ga., 287, 315
Ann Arbor, Mich., 17
Antietam, Md., 240, 252
Appomattox Court House, Va., 10, 12, 86, 117
Appomattox River, 56
Aquia Creek Landing, Va., *65,* 70
Arlington National Cemetery, *302, 303*
armies, supplies for, 39–44
Armistead & White, 50
Army of Northern Virginia, 115–116, 117
Army of Tennessee (Confederate), 204
Army of the Potomac, 115, *119,* 167, 169; supplies for, *65, 70, 74, 77*
arsenals, 42, *46,* 119
artillery, 113–115, 117, 118, *120–132, 154–157,* 240
Atlanta, Ga., 51, *241, 258, 294, 310*
Atlanta (ironclad), *66*
Atlanta & West Point Railroad, 51
Atlantic & North Carolina Railroad, 62
Auden, W. H., 8
Augusta, Ga., 42, *47*
Augusta Powder Works, *47*

bakery, *106*
Baltimore, Md., 113
bands, *181–183, 191*
Bankes, T. W., *293*
Bank of Richmond, *30*
banks, *30, 278*
Banks, Nathaniel, *308*
Barnard, George, 51, 158, 259
Barnum, Henry A., *248*
Barton, Clara, 205, 315
Baton Rouge, La., *292*
Battery (Charleston, S.C.), *270*
Battery Gregg, 143
Battery Hays, *124*
Battery Marion, *126*
Battery Wagner, 117
Beacon House (South Carolina), *256*
Bealton, Va., 57

Beaufort, S.C., *83, 219*
Beauregard, P. G. T., *204, 212*
Belle Isle, Va., *285, 288*
Belle Plain, Va., *283*
Benavides, Cristobal, *207*
Benavides, Refugio, *207*
Benjamin, Judah, 203, *210*
Bermuda Hundred, Va., *84*
blacks: emancipation of, 8–11, 22, 242, 253; as slaves, 8–11, 22; as soldiers, 23, 40, *104,* 203–204, *214–222*
blacksmith shops, *95, 97, 180*
"Bloody Angle" (Spotsylvania, Va.), 116
Boone's Knob, Ky., *89*
Borden, Gail, 41
Bostwick Brothers, *76*
Botts, John Minor, *31*
Bowker, Isaiah, *288*
Boyd, Belle, 205
Brandy Station, Va., *76, 85*
Breckinridge, John C., *215*
Bridgeport, Conn., *25*
Bridgeport (Conn.) *Weekly Farmer,* 25
bridges, *62, 63, 90, 273*
Broad Street (Charleston, S.C.), *264*
Brockenbrough house (Richmond), *29*
Brown, Joseph, 33
Browne, William, 203
Brownsville, Tex., *207*
Buchanan, James, 8, 16
Buck, Silas, *325*
buildings. *See* public buildings
Bull Run, Va., 40, *163, 164, 292*
Burnside's Rhode Island Zouaves, *186, 190*

Cameron, Simon, 43, *55*
Camp Chase Prison (Ohio), *290*
Camp Nelson, Ky., *90–110*
Camp Sumter (Georgia), 287
Capitol (U.S.), *14, 19, 26*
carpenters' shop, *97*
Cary Street (Richmond, Va.), *275*
Cashier, Albert, *224*
casualties, 239–240, *244–248, 250–252, 293*
Catherine Furnace (Chancellorsville, Va.), 115
Catlett's Station, Va., 60
cavalry, *79–80,* 100, *102, 188, 199;* 1st New York, *177;* Kentucky Confederate, *321;* Rush's Lancers, *184;* 16th Confederate, *325;* 33d

Texas, *207*
Cavalry Bureau (U.S.), 79
Cedar Creek, Va., *175*
Cedar Mountain, Va., *50,* 114
cemeteries, *269, 291, 292, 302–306, 309*
Centreville, Va., *147*
Chancellorsville, Va., 70, 115
Charleston, S.C.: destruction in, *138–140, 260–270;* forts around, 8, 113, 123, *126, 127, 138–140, 146,* 211
Charlotte, N.C., 42
Chattanooga, Tenn., *51,* 58, *63,* 79, *122,* 315
Cherokee Mounted Rifles, 206
Chicago, Ill., 41
Christian Commission, U.S., 205, *232, 233*
churches, *262, 265, 266, 269*
Circular Church (Charleston, S.C.), *262, 269*
City Point, Va., *69, 72, 77, 81,* 226
Clalin, Francis, *222, 223*
Cleburne, Patrick R., 203, 204, *209*
Clemenceau, Georges, 7
Cobb's Hill, Va., 56
Cold Harbor, Va., 240
Columbia, S.C., 242, *259*
commissary depots, *75–77*
Conduct of the War Committee, 11
convalescent camp, 108
Cook, George S., 139
Cooley, Samuel, 75, 79, 219
Cooper River, *146*
Corinth, Miss., *50,* 168
Crowley, Mike, *179*
Cumberland River, 116
Cushing, Alonzo H., 115
Custer, George A., *307*
Customs House (New York City), *20*

Dahlgren, John A., 203, *211*
Davis, Jefferson, *27, 215;* leadership of, 8, 10, 34, 201; opposition to, 31, 32, 33, 34; policies of, 11, 28, 204; residence of, *29*
Debow's Review, 42
Detroit, Mich., 17
Dilger, Hubert, 114–115
disease, 240
Dix, Dorothea, 205
Donaldsonville, La., *255*
Douglas, Stephen, *16*
Drayton, Thomas, 22

Drew, John, *206*
Drewry's Bluff, Va., 117
Dry Tortugas, Fla., *133*
Duane, Harriet, 226
D'Utassy, Fredcrick G., *213*

Edmonds, Emma E., 205
Edwards, Jay D., 21
8th Pennsylvania Reserves, *195*
83d Pennsylvania, *186*
El Cid (ship), 68
emancipation, 8–11, 22
Emancipation Oak, *22*
Emancipation Proclamation, 22, 203, 204
Emerson, Ralph Waldo, 11
Engle & Furlong, 287
Ericsson, John, 203
"Eruptive Hospital," *109*
Etowah River, 63

Fairfax Court House, Va., *73*
Farragut, David G., *306*
Fauquier Springs (Va.) Hotel, *257*
Ferguson, Tom, *215*
V Corps (Union), *71*
52d U.S. Colored Infantry, *166*
56th Massachusetts, *165*
1st Michigan, *17*
1st New York Artillery, *150*
1st New York Cavalry, *177*
1st South Carolina Volunteers, 23
1st U.S. Colored Infantry, *220*
1st U.S. Sharpshooters, *178*
Five Civilized Tribes, 201, 206
forage shop, *96*
Forrest, Nathan Bedford, 222
Fort Bartow, *320*
Fort Carroll, 113
Fort Columbus, *132*
Fort Damnation, 153
Fort Donelson, 116
Fort Fisher, 117, *127,* 149
Fort Gaines, 117
Fort Hamilton, 113
Fort Hell, 117
Fort Henry, 116
fortifications, 116–118, *133–158;* field, 116–118, *141–154*
Fort Jackson, 117
Fort Jefferson, *133, 134*
Fort Mahone, 153
Fort Monroe, 113, *133,* 246
Fort Morgan, 117, *126, 137*

Fort Moultrie, *126, 138, 254*
Fort Pickens, 21
Fort Pillow, 204, 222
Fort Powell, 117
Fort Pulaski, 113, 116, *136*
Fort Putnam, *123, 124, 143*
Fort Rice, 153
Fort Saint Philip, 117
Fort Sanders, 117
Fort Stedman, 117
Fort Stevens, *121*
Fort Sumter, *134*; destruction of, 117, 124, *139–140, 158, 211, 298, 299*; surrender of, 8, 12, *13*, 113
41st Georgia, *322*
41st Illinois, 218
46th Indiana, *185*
47th Illinois, *167*
Franklin, Tenn., 209
Franklin Paper Mill (Richmond, Va.), *273*
Franklin Pike, *82*
Fredericksburg, Va., 115, 116, 240, 241
Freedmen's Bureau, 242
French & Company, 166

Gainesville, Ga., *309*
Gallego Flour Mills (Richmond, Va.), *280*
Gardner, Alexander, *14*, 272, 280, 297
Garibaldi Guard, 213
General (railroad engine), *315*
Gentry, Watson M., *247*
Georgia Railroad, 51
Gettysburg, Pa., *294, 301, 316, 322*; battle of, 10, *26*, 115, 239, 240, 241, *252*
Gibbon, John, *297*
Giesboro Point (near Washington, D.C.), 80
Gillmore, Quincy A., 116
Gloucester Point, Va., *128*
Gordon, John B., funeral of, *310–311*
Gorgas, Josiah, 115
Goslin's Zouaves, *185*
grain sheds, *103*
Grant, Ulysses S., 90, 116, 236, 300, *306*; death of, *312–314*; and siege of Petersburg, 69, 72
Greenhow, Rose O'Neal, 204
Green Island, Ga., *320*
Griswold, M. M., *290*

Haas & Peale, *123, 124, 143, 150*
Hampton Roads, Va., *133*

Harpers Ferry, Va., *177*
Harpers Ferry Armory, 52
Haupt, Herman, 43, 61, 62, 63
Haxall & Crenshaw's, *45*
Hayes, Joseph, 35
Hazel Grove (Chancellorsville, Va.), 115
Hazel River, 180
Hazlett, Charles E., 115
Head, Truman, *178*
Heywood, J. D., 62
Hickman Bridge (Camp Nelson, Ky.), *90*
Hilton Head Island, S.C., *22, 75, 78, 79, 173*
Hodgers, Jennie, *224*
Hollywood Cemetery (Richmond, Va.), *291, 306*
Hooker, Joseph ("Fighting Joe"), 70, 73, 115, 318
hospitals, *84, 108, 109*, 228, 249
Hotze, Henry, 203
houses, *29, 32*
Houston, F. K., *13*
howitzers, 113–114, *120*
Hunt, Henry J., 115
Huntsville, Tex., *284*

immigrants, 202–203, *208–213*
Index (newspaper), 203
Indians, 201–202, 206
industry, 40–41, 42, *45–49, 52–54*
inflation, 30
inspection yard, *100*
inventions, 41
Irish Brigade of the West, *210*
Iron Brigade, 194
Irwinville, Ga., 34

Jackson, Thomas J. ("Stonewall"), 114, 115, 205
Jackson Mine (Michigan), 55
James, Charles T., 114
James River, *45*, 66, 117, *132*
James River Canal, *45*
Johnson, Adam R., *248*
Johnson, Andrew, 9
Joslyn & Smith, *319*

Kentucky Confederate Cavalry, *321*
Kentucky River, 89, 91
Kentucky State Guard, *161*
Knoxville, Tenn., 117

Knoxville (Tenn.) Deaf and Dumb Asylum, *169*

Lee, Robert E., 90, 113, 115, 116, 309; defeat of, 10, 44, 86, 117; lack of supplies and, 44, 114; surrender by, 10, 236
Letcher, John, 33
Levy & Cohen, 45
Lexington, Mo., 141
Libby Prison (Richmond, Va.), *285, 286*
Lincoln, Abraham, 9, 10, *14*, 24, 201, 242; death of, 19; Emancipation Proclamation of, 22, 204; support for, 11, 12, 15, 16, 17, 26, 208
Linn, Royan, *319*
Little Bighorn (Montana), *307*
Little Round Top (Gettysburg, Pa.), *26*, 115
Longstreet, James, 117, 309
Lookout Mountain (Chattanooga, Tenn.), *58, 189, 319*
Louis-Napoléon, 114
Lowell Light Infantry, *162*
loyalty oaths, 10, 24
Lynchburg, Va., 117

McCallum, Daniel C., 62
McCormick, Cyrus, 41
machine shop, *98*
Macon, Ga., *48, 49*
Mallet, John, 203
Mallory, Stephen, 203
Manassas, Va., *300*
Manchester, Va., *45*
Martland, W. J., *181*
Martz, D. H. Lee, *324*
Meigs, Montgomery C., *14*
Memminger, Christopher, 203
Memphis, Tenn., *249*
Mexican-Americans, 202, 207
Military Telegraph Corps, *57–58*
militiamen, *161–198*
Milliken's Bend, La., 204
mining, 55
Missionary Ridge (Chattanooga, Tenn.), 122
Mississippi River, 148
Mobile, Ala., 117
Mobile Bay, 137
Monitor (ironclad), 203
Montezuma Regiment, 164

Montgomery, Ala., *27*
monuments, *300–305, 307, 316–318*
Moore, A. B., 42
Moore, H. P., 21
Moore, Ned, 114
Morgan, John Hunt, *321*
Morgantown, W.Va., *163*
Morris Island, S.C., *135, 143, 150–152*
Mount McGregor, N.Y., *312*
mule chute, *101*
Mulligan, James A., *210*

napoleons, 114, 118, *121, 122*
Nashville, Tenn., 42, 51, 82
National Lancers, *162*
New Bern, N.C., *219*
New Creek, Va., *210*
New Haven, Conn., 41
New Orleans, La., 10, 42, 117, *291*
New York City, *20, 25*, 113, *132, 313–314*
New York Fire Zouaves, *193*
New York Sanitary Fair, 231
IX Corps (Union), 82
95th Illinois, 224
95th Pennsylvania, *185*
Northeastern Railroad Depot (Charleston, S.C.), *270*

officers' headquarters, *90*
124th Illinois, 166
Orange & Alexandria Railroad, 60
Orange Turnpike, 115
ordnance storehouse and yard, *78, 93*
Osborn & Durbec, *134, 135*
O'Sullivan, Timothy, 50, *128, 149*
Otero, Miguel Antonio, Sr., 202

Palmito Ranch, Tex., *221*
Pamunkey River, *64*
Parker, Ely S., *236*
Parrott, Robert P., 114
Patent Office (U.S.), *20*
Peabody, George, *306*
Peabody Fund, 306
Pea Ridge, Ark., 202
Pegram, Willie, 115
Pelham, John, 115
Pember, Phoebe, 205
Pemberton, John C., 300
Pendleton, William Nelson, 115
Pensacola, Fla., 21

Petersburg, Va., 117, 253; destruction in, 256, 271; siege of, 69, 72, 122, 128, 204; Union army in, 56, 85, 149, 150, 153, 220
Peyton, George Q., 116
Philadelphia, Pa., 41
Pickett, George E., 115, 241
Pike, Albert, 201, 202, 206
Planter (steamer), 203, 214
Point Lookout (Chattanooga, Tenn.), 189. See also Lookout Mountain
Polignac, Camille Armand Jules Marie, Prince de, 203, 212
Port Hudson, La., 148, 204, 255, 283
Port Royal, S.C., 23
Portsmouth, N.H., 21
Potomac River, 80
Price, Sterling, 141
prisons/prison camps, 107, 283–290
Prometheus (transport ship), 68
provost marshal's office, 107
public buildings, 20, 29, 33, 51, 85, 294; Capitol (U.S.), 14, 19, 26; destruction of, 262, 271; Secession Hall, 27, 262; Virginia State House, 29, 271

Quintero, Juan, 202

railroads, 43–44, 51, 59–63, 278, 315
Rains, George Washington, 47
Rapidan River, 242
Rappahannock River, 76, 147
Red Cross, 205
Rees, David R., 285
reservoirs, 91, 92
reunions, 321–325
Reynolds, John F., 316
Rhett, Robert Barnwell, 32
Rhett House, 32
Rhode Island Zouaves, 186, 190
Richmond, Va., 291; artillery in, 125, 155; Christian Commission in, 230, 232; Confederates in, 28–29, 30, 52, 116, 117, 204; destruction in, 271–280; industry in, 42, 45, 46; reunions in, 323–325; soldiers' home in, 324
Richmond & Petersburg Railroad bridge, 273
Richmond Armory and Arsenal, 42, 46
Richmond Enquirer, 42

Riddle, A. J., 287
rifled artillery, 114, 115, 116, 118, 122–126, 142, 240
rifles, 187, 188, 190, 191, 240
Rio Grande, 207
Ripetti, Alexander, 213
Robertson Hospital (Richmond, Va.), 228
Rochester, N.Y., 184
Rock Island Prison Camp (Illinois), 290
Rocky Face Ridge, Ga., 75
Rose, John, 289
Ross, John, 202
Rush's Lancers, 184
Russell, A. J., 59, 77

Saltville, Va., 204
saltwater condenser, 83
Sanitary Commission, U.S., 205, 230–232
Savage Station, Va., 245
Savannah, Ga., 113, 136, 241, 259, 320
sawmill, 98
Schofield's Iron Works, 49
Schurz, Carl, 208
Scott, Winfield, 303
Secession Hall (Charleston, S.C.), 27, 262
Selma, Ala., 42
7th New York Militia, 25
71st New York Militia, 164
Seward, William, 15
Shenandoah Valley campaign, 44
Shepherdstown, W.Va., 305
Sheridan, Philip H., 44, 243
Sherman, William Tecumseh, 43, 63, 75, 241–242
Shiloh, Tenn., 240
ships, 21, 64–69, 214, 293
shipyards, 41, 45
Sibley, Henry Hopkins, 207
Sigel, Franz, 208
Signal Corps, 56–58
VI Corps (Union), 74, 180
6th Pennsylvania Cavalry, 184
16th Confederate Cavalry, 325
16th Pennsylvania, 248
62d U.S. Colored Infantry, 221
69th New York, 163
slaves, 22; emancipation of, 8–11, 22, 242, 253; as soldiers, 23, 40. See also blacks
Slidell, John, 31
Smalls, Robert, 203, 214

Smith, Josh, 290
Smith, W. M., 121
Smith, William, 33
Smith, William M., 288
soldiers' homes, 110, 324
Soldiers' National Monument (Gettysburg, Pa.), 301
South Atlantic Blockading Squadron, 211
Spotsylvania, Va., 116
stables, 79, 80, 102
Stahel, Julius, 203
Stanton, Edwin M., 16
Stephens, Alexander H., 34
Stevens, Thaddeus, 15
stockade, 107
Stoneman's Station, Va., 76
Streight, Abel D., 286
Stuart, J. E. B., 306
Sullivans Island, S.C., 138
Sultana (steamer), 293
Sumner, Charles, 15
Swasey, Charles H., 302
Sweeny, Thomas W., 209

Taft, William H., 316
Taunton, Mass., 302
telegraph, 43, 56–58
Tennessee River, 63, 116
Tennessee State House (Chattanooga), 51
10th Virginia, 324
Terry's Texas Rangers, 307
Texas State Penitentiary (Huntsville), 284
3d Kansas Light Artillery, 120
3d Massachusetts Heavy Artillery, 121
3d New Hampshire, 173
Thirteenth Amendment, 12
31st New York, 164
31st Pennsylvania, 165
33d New Jersey, 198
33d Texas Cavalry, 207
34th Massachusetts, 175
39th New York, 213
Thorne (transport ship), 68
Tompkins, Sally, 205, 228
transportation systems, 40, 43–44, 51, 59–69. See also railroads; ships
Tredegar Iron Works (Richmond, Va.), 42, 44, 46, 279
12th Massachusetts, 179
22d New York, 177

22d Ohio, 168
23d Illinois, 210

U.S. Christian Commission, 205, 232, 233
U.S. Customs House (Richmond, Va.), 29
U.S. Military Railroad, 61, 62
U.S. Sanitary Commission, 205, 230–232

Vallandigham, Clement L., 24
Vallejo, Salvador, 202
Vance, Zebulon, 33
Vandalia (ship), 21
Vanderhoff's Wharf (Charleston, S.C.), 146
Van Lew, Elizabeth, 204
Vicksburg, Miss., 10, 30, 166, 169, 204, 300, 319
Vidaurri, Atanacio, 207
Vidaurri, Santiago, 202
Virginia governor's mansion, 33
Virginia Military Institute, 282
Virginia State Arsenal, 42, 46
Virginia State House (Richmond), 29, 271

wagon yard, 99
Walker, Mary, 205
Waltham, Mass., 308
Ward, Durbin, 11
warehouses, 105
Washington, D.C., 14, 18, 19, 26, 56
Washington Arsenal, 119
Washington Photograph Gallery (Vicksburg, Miss.), 319
Washington U.S. Military General Hospital, 249
Watie, Stand, 202
Webster U.S. Military General Hospital, 249
Wells, George D., 175
Western & Atlantic Railroad engine, 315
Whistler, Ala., 325
White House Landing, Va., 64, 233
White's Ranch, Tex., 221
Wilmington, N.C., 117, 127, 149
Winder, John, 284
women, war efforts of, 204–205, 223–235

York River, 142
Yorktown, Va., 128, 141, 142

zouaves, 184–186, 193